Josep Miquel Sobrer

THE BOOK OF ORACLES or A POET'S TAROT

First published in Catalan by Edicions de la Magrana, 1988. First published in English by Spitting Frog in 1994

First translated into English by Josep Miquel Sobrer 1994

Photo of Josep Miquel Sobrer taken by David Pace

Editorial Director: Darren Shill
Art Director: Kay Medaglia
Editor: Tori Jones
Designers: Fez Inkwright and Jing Lau
Cover Design: Fez Inkwright

Printed in China

ISBN: 978-1-912634-54-5

10 9 8 7 6 5 4 3 2 1

www.liminal11.com

CONTENTS

•

INTRODUCTION

•

The first English language edition of *The Book of Oracles or A Poet's Tarot* was published in the spring of 1994. The book, by Josep Miquel "Pep" Sobrer, was published by a vanity press, The Spitting Frog Press, also created by Pep. Pep wrote this book through our courtship. In fact, I have a very charming letter explaining his trepidations over our getting married, even though I had yet to answer the question, *"Will you marry me?"*, on the back side of pages from an earlier draft of the book (the Five and Six of Cups).

From the very start of our marriage, there were at least four cases of books in our basement; then three cases in the garage of our new home, a large space necessitated by the arrival of my third child, Pep's first and only son, Miró; then back to the basement went two cases when we moved to a smaller home when our two older children, Greer and Ryland McIntyre, had grown and were creating homes of their own.

Life and its relentless demands left the cases more or less forgotten in our basement. Then Pep was contacted by Melissa Cynova, the author of *Kitchen Table Tarot,* who also wrote a blog about the Tarot. Melissa wanted to interview Pep about his book. I remember Pep being very excited about the interview, and afterwards he felt encouraged to try selling the remaining books online as well as to see about a second publishing of his book. Unfortunately, right on the heels of his talk with Melissa, it was determined that Pep's cancer, diagnosed four years earlier as metastatic colon cancer, had spread to his brain, affecting his motor skills so that he could no longer physically write. Within five months, on January 1st, 2015, my beloved husband died.

In classic Pep style, he wrote his own obituary a few months before he died. His obituary caused a small stir in Bloomington, Indiana where we lived, and also in Barcelona, Spain, his home city, where a couple of the newspapers translated and published his obituary: *"The writer who writes his own obituary."* In that obituary, Pep suggests you read *A Poet's Tarot*. Suddenly I was besieged by requests from friends and strangers: could they borrow, or buy, a copy of the book from me? In the foggy days after Pep's death I could not find those two cases. Anywhere. I went through every part of the house, and they were nowhere to be found. The handful of copies that I did find were quickly claimed by myself and our children to keep as our own. I searched through Pep's personal files hoping to find the original manuscript or at least a computer file, instead I found a copy of a letter Pep intended to send to a publisher to see about a second publication of his book. In that letter, he notes that the original manuscript was lost, but he could easily reproduce one if interest warranted the effort.

So began my own journey to retype and recreate the manuscript. I know that I could have scanned the book, but I wanted to honor Pep, who would have retyped over scanning. The typing and careful reading brings you closer to the text. With the exception of a few small edits, the following book is the same as the original, *The Book of Oracles or A Poet's Tarot.*

Pep did not have a dedication for his first book, but I think if he could have rewritten his manuscript he would have included one for the second publication. I think it would go something like this:

For my son, Miró Henry Sobrer

Remember Ithaka

~Francesca Sobrer

PREFACE: HOW TO READ THIS BOOK

•

This is a book about the drama of self-awareness. Just as a person is made up of many, each of us being a brew of internalized characters, so is this book made up by the many voices from that drama. I call its pieces 'oracles', from the Latin *oraculum* (which derives from *os*, 'mouth'), because in them I have allowed the voices of those many to speak through me, much as I imagine the ancient oracles interpreted the meanings of their gods.

These oracles are organized following the structure and symbolism of Tarot cards. They are my verbal interpretations of the cards. The value of the Tarot is relative to the questions with which we approach the cards and to our willingness to see ourselves reflected in that unusual mirror. And so it is with this *Book of Oracles*, which is a guide to finding those questions, just as much as an interpretation of the cards and whatever may lie behind them.

The author recommends two ways of reading this book: one straight and one combinative. The straight reading follows the order of presentation and proposes an organic architecture of the whole. It begins with the Lesser Secrets and moves on to the Greater Secrets. An essay at the end presents a rational view of the whole topic, of the Tarot and of the book itself. The Lesser Secrets are divided, as are the cards, into four traditional suits: Clubs deal with the physical worlds, Cups with the world of emotions, Swords with the political world of the mind, and Golds with the world of the spirit. Although less advisory, because they have to do with psychological archetypes rather than situations, the Greater Secrets are also presented in a traditional sequence.

The other recommended way of reading is combinative and aleatory, and for that the reader will need a deck of cards. The idea here is to pick a random card or cards and read the corresponding oracle. Before you purchase a pack of Tarot cards you may start with a regular deck of cards, such as the ones used for playing poker or bridge. To do this all you need to know is the following correspondence: what this book calls Clubs correspond to Clubs, Cups to Hearts, Swords to Spades, and Golds to Diamonds. The final essay explains in detail a method for drawing the cards and the reasons for the above admonitions.

Self-exploration should not be rushed. Nor can it be approached mechanically. Ultimately the Tarot speaks through its images to your intuition. These oracles should also speak to your intuition; being verbal, they may more readily stimulate the reader's imagination than the silent cards. Feel the freedom of your mind whenever you read them. To advance along the road proposed here you must be flexible. Be open, be patient, and be playful. Let yourself be in this book and in the cards. Approach the oracles with your questions or your skepticism; carry on a dialogue with them. These oracles should be seen as open messages, as the springboards to your own imagination, as the staircase for the descent into the deeper regions of your self. Each one of the pieces for the Lesser Secrets has two distinct parts which complement each other dynamically. In some cases, the two parts are contrary options; in most cases one part voices the advice the card has to offer while the other presents a vision to help the reader imagine.

One word of caution. The Tarot is not for the weak-hearted, and this book offers no sugar-coating. You must be ready to face issues such as death and evil, in others as much as in yourself. You must be ready to defy comfort as well as folly, you must accept that the picture of yourself is not always a pretty one. Rise to your aspirations and sink to your fears. We all have inner monsters who we must meet if we are to grow; and there is something divine in all of us. The road may be difficult, but the arrival is worthwhile. You may start with the courage to face the unknown. May this book be your traveling companion.

A note from Francesca: While reading this book, you may notice the rather perplexing absence of the tens. In his notes on the Tarot at the end of the book, Pep points out that he used a Spanish pack of cards that only had 12 cards per suit. He added the Queens back into the deck, but he left the tens out. My son Miró suggests that if you should draw a ten and are looking for the corresponding oracle then substitute with the Page card. My daughter Greer, an aspiring reader of the Tarot, supposes that the absence of the tens is because the tens are all about the "Three C's": culmination, complexity and completion. She proposes that they are the maximum expression of their suit, and Pep left them out for the reader to determine for themselves, after having read the rest, what the culmination of the suit means to them personally. I can hear Pep saying: "As you will."

THE LESSER SECRETS

I

ACE OF CLUBS

•

This is where we begin, with our power, with our bodies. Feet well planted on the ground, weight distributed evenly, muscles without tension, our strength a living thing. As we breathe, the world around us comes into focus as if everything we see were paying attention to us.

We have found the present.

And in the present we have found our strength: this moment of gravitating suspension, this weightless rootedness, this ever changing timeless now. This here that is everywhere, this balance on the crest of time. Here our worries will crumble into past or future. Here our suffering becomes our experience, our needs become our wants, and our fears open up into our hope. Here our friends and our enemies reflect the alien light of our sobriety; for it is here, and now, that we see them all, each with a will of his or her own, locked in the ravels of their time. And we stand between yesterday and tomorrow, those two phantoms of nothingness. We are. We feel our power, our reality. Our hunger no stronger than our jaws, our heart no weaker than our challenge.

This is the gift we call life.

•

As you start on your new journey you must learn to speak out. Speak out in the honest language of your quest. Start with the word No. A simple, wrathless, even joyful No. People may be beseeching you; do not judge them, but do not rush to their rescue. Let them have their needs; you have yours. Think of your power as a hand holding a bat, and think you are hitting those balls tossed at you that belong elsewhere. Whack them away. Say: "No."

To ill daring, a good whack. To the enemy within you, a whack. To the enemy before you, "No." To the fear of nightmares, a whack.

Squeeze your club, lift it. Squint a little as you fix your eyes on your objective and, as you deliver the blow, let out the roar of the tension you had locked up in your chest.

A stroke with the club. To those who have deceived you, to those who have abused you, to those who have betrayed you.

A good blow with the club!

To those who have robbed you, and have insulted you, and have wounded you. To all of them. To each one of them: young and old, men and women.

A wallop with the club!

TWO OF CLUBS

•

Who am I?

I am one with a mask. My mask, for all its contortions, makes a set fixed face. Yet, knowing it is fixed, I feel liberated by my mask. It is as if I were nothing more than the space between my skin and the mask—between my body and its projection—the space that makes me aware of my inner emptiness, of how I have tried to fill that emptiness with the retinue of contortions of my mask: with my smiles, my grimaces, the thousand fantasies my face can bear. Yes, this is where my self lies: between the many senses of my striving ego (my grins and all my needy roles), and that planetary mass of inner uncertainty.

My mask deceived no one but me. Aware, I am ready to face my inner emptiness, the unfathomed, timeless, divine emptiness of my humanity.

•

Sometimes the possibility of choice makes us lose our head.

We have the world in our hands and the scepter of the dominion of time, and yet we are ready to throw it away, to throw away not only one item of our wealth, but the whole lot.

We worry: Ah—we think—if we hadn't been given this option! If we could return to the pristine path we didn't take! If we could live each day twice: once as we have lived it, and another once as we think we should have lived it. One day for our heart, one day for our mind... But both would be lost. The clock ticks, we think the pendulum knows time. The rose wilts and we think it dies; we decay and think we aspire. Those are our sins that have rent us asunder.

It is inevitable: we feel cheated by the world. We feel the play is coming to an end and we are just as afraid of the silence to follow the performances as of the applause. Curtain!

THREE OF CLUBS

•

We have lost the art of looking out the window, of seeing how the branches in bloom sway to the rhythm of the breeze, how the street shines after a shower. Of just looking, like we do in stores, but in life.

Whenever we look out the window, the people we see give us pleasure. Our eyes follow that youth walking with an unusual gait, the overflowing basket of the woman who is on her way back from market, the old man leaning on his cane, a primped businesswoman drumming on the sidewalk with her dressy shoes, some workers in monkey suits. They all look so timeless, from our post at the window; we might think they will never age or change, never die. From our window we do not see—we do not care to see—the passage of time, the weight of life's changes. The world appears so very light from our window on the street. Everyone seems a part of an animated film, to be viewed again and again.

We may also be eternal when, lifting our head from our worry, we show up at the window to just look out, an undecipherable face drinking in the world.

•

Three is for complication. It is the first number that allows us to become entangled. One goes this way, two goes that way; three may disagree with both and entice them to quarrel. Three are the dimensions of reality – and of chaos. But the three clubs could also build a harmony. These clubs can team up, stack up, play. A multiple and social relationship.

Business, market, society... These are all tangos that take three. Consider the market: the merchant comes to intercede between the other two, the farmer and the bureaucrat. You want one thing, she wants another thing—in the third you may find your intercessor. Also your betrayer.

Riddle of this card upside down: business, success, possible complications.

FOUR OF CLUBS

•

The year begins with the rains. The year's beginning is a return to equilibrium, to life, to the persistent tottering of existence. The raindrops sparkle on leaves that thirst for life, slide down the stem. The arid world drinks up the cold water of a gray day.

Meanwhile, we celebrate with unleavened bread our exodus from winter, from the dark exile within ourselves, and renew our forgetfulness with songs of history and the taste of bitter herbs. We flee slavery, any slavery, all slavery.

We break the four walls of our prison and come out to let the wind in the open fields be our guide.

•

But freedom is not always a blessing. Freedom turns to wandering, wandering to perplexity, perplexity to loss. The monotony of the open sky becomes your new labyrinth. The trusted guide cannot lead you into yourself, while the more you seek your true nature the easier you'll forget that what's within you can be found nowhere else.

Or you may disguise your freedom as a reaction, make it into a burden of defiant prerogatives. Protecting your freedom against itself, you may turn down requests you fear would limit it, and wiggle yourself out of contracts, anchor your soul in refusal. Or you could take your four clubs and set up a golden cage to keep your freedom unpolluted. Do not barter the wind for a whirl of tight-fisted randomness.

FIVE OF CLUBS

•

I set down four of the sticks and thus build my secret chamber. In it, all alone, I stand holding my fifth club.

In the lonely chamber I begin flogging myself.
Because I feel guilty.
Because I said no.
Because he would give up everything for me, he said.
She sees everything so clearly...
You're the one at fault, he said.
Why are you leaving me? she moans.
And I lash myself.
If I leave, a lashing; if I remain, a lashing.
All alone with my club inside my four walls. I need nothing else. The shame is all mine.

•

The club locked inside the other four is the inimical giant we all have within ourselves. Strong and mighty, this giant. Our dark father, the tenebrous god who stands in judgment, whose condemnation is as terrible as it is dispassionate. Cigar-smoking and foul-tongued, this judge sees everything and allows for no atonement.

Only one thing we can do: open up the four walls of our wooden house and look again in the cold light at this dusky and powerful father we had begotten in our fears.

SIX OF CLUBS

•

You must trust your power because sooner or later all things will come to rest in their proper place. The trees need no advice to put forth leaves, and nobody gave the nightingale singing lessons. You were not put on this earth to waste away. The best hit is not always the one that follows anguished premeditation.

Remember you are not alone. If at times you feel lonely, if everything that touches you seems about to crack and threatens to separate you from yourself and abandon you to the loveless desert of your loneliness, remember that in truth few things break apart. Things hold. And we all have enough might to move on. Our success is assured. The triumphal procession can now be planned.

Remember your parents and your children, and your siblings and your lovers. How rich you all are! They are enriched by what you have given them, and you have the wealth of your strength and your giving. The procession may begin. Accept all compliments.

•

When your powers are matched by those of your opponent, stay calm. Do not rush into action. Learn to distinguish between patience and postponement, find your reality in your tempered breathing. This present may be for you a difficult moment, even though you know it won't last forever. Stay with it all the same.

Feel the indefinite delay. Patience is the secret weapon you now need. Be in no hurry. Do not forget that the immobility of the universe is always illusory. Everything walks inevitably towards death, which is the beginning of otherness.

Beware of the rash call to action. Do not delude your spirit with desperate motion. Your actions must feel right. Tread lightly, walk serenely until then, and beyond.

The frustration of the moment should help you understand the value of waiting, of unresolved situations. For life is all irresolution.

SEVEN OF CLUBS

•

A wedge, just a little piece of wood, a modest stick may succeed in separating the elements that need to be separated. It may also give you the strength you need. It may help you jump over the fence, prop up a faulty wall, secure a crucial door... Or it may give you the chimeric impression you can check all the other forces assailing you.

In order to know what kind of club you hold—if it is a barrier, a wedge, a pulley, or the weapon of your opponent—look at your hands. Stop for an instant and find out whether your fists are gripping the wood with rage, or whether you are handling the club with the dexterity of a surgeon holding the scalpel, or clutching it with the calloused devotion of a gardener's hands on a mattock.

There is a patchy fog this morning, eager to be broken down by the sun. No point in your blowing hard to disperse it.

•

Yes, look at you, both hands on your club and battling your six opponents. They have you cornered and there you stand, besieged, atop the mound of your righteousness. "They shall not pass," you tell yourself with clenched teeth. How strong you are, how determinate, all fired up. You are a soldier of reason, the avenger of truth.

Has it occurred to you that every single one of your six opponents is grasping the club with the same holy desperation? That they all feel they are the right defenders of an unpopular but just cause? That, like you, they all crave the battle because it makes them feel important, and heroic, and righteous?

You could plant your club next to theirs, and let them be, as they will let you be. But first you must try to know who they are, and whence they come.

EIGHT OF CLUBS

•

The end of the journey grows nearer. Days have grown longer. The river seems steady in its valley now, approaching the sea. The sky is blue and fills at dusk with the shrieking of birds. There is no hurry. The project I have in my hands is well thought-out and strong. My goal is clear, the end in sight.

Time for a pause, and time to think of love. Better: rather than thinking, it is time for loving. For loving with strength and loving out of strength.

The valley is green. A clump of trees offers its shade to today's travelers. Atop the hill a stone hut bursts in the western sunlight. The adventures and the perils of my journey are behind me. Yet nothing has ended.

•

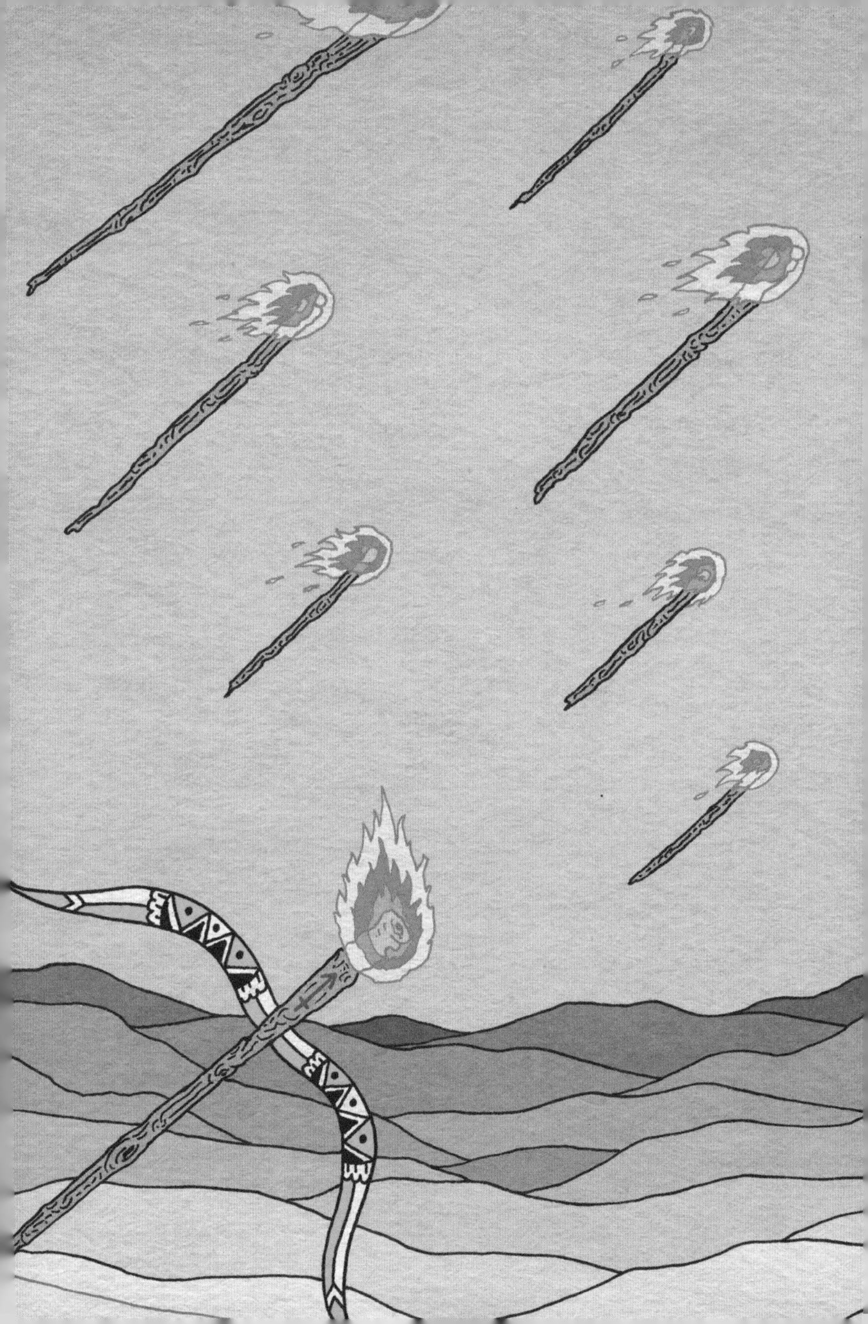

At times we have so much that our lives become complicated. We struggle, we stumble, and in general annoy each other. It doesn't matter what we have or what we need; we want more. Abundance spurs us. A gentle scarcity would be beneficial to our souls, but we are moved by our inner hunger to crave for more, more, more.

Jealousy is born of abundance: too many things, too much noise. What are you doing and what shall I do?

What are you doing whenever I do not see you? What have you done?

Too many questions and too much curiosity.
Too much prevention and too much fear.
And for this we have worked so hard?

NINE OF CLUBS

•

We often grip only one of our strengths and mistrust all the others which appear to us opposing the chosen one. They are so many, we tell ourselves, so many; we couldn't possibly be so richly endowed. Surely so much wealth cannot be ours...

And yet, here it is: our strength. Potent and erect. Assured, varied, and well set on the ground.

We'll have no reason to fear if we accept the eight weapons never before used.

•

Be alert and get ready because, all told, you are alone in the world. Pay no notice to what those around you say. Listen to their words, for many do love you, but do not lose sight of your self. Seek completion in your own soul rather than in the company of lovers, for you shall never taste love so sweet as when you yourself have come into full bloom.

And good advice—guidance appearing ever so reasonable, sounding ever so just—must be considered with the greatest care. Do not go gentle into good advice. What seems most logical and natural should be reflected upon with the most unyielding eye. You will have to rethink the present project, advanced as it is. Sleep on it. Let your dreams show it to you afresh, with the starkness of the absurd. See it then, out of place, peopled by monsters, beating with the blood of turbulence.

PAGE OF CLUBS

•

You have reached the culmination of your doing. Don't you see yourself, right now? You stand, an intense expression on your face, a club in your hand, ready. Ready for work, for doing, for leaving your traces, for furrowing the world with your might.

A life of organization and work, yours, of enterprise, a job well done. All you have produced: the objects you have polished, the actions you have organized, the animals you have trained, the books you have read. You believe that your being is your doing, that your work is what matters.

But at the same time, now, something made you stop. Being and doing... A perplexity creeps in: where is all your being? Is there something you can do to be more yourself? This perplexity takes you to the heart of the matter.

•

There are truths and there are errors. I feel the tension in my legs, in my body. Am I condemned to this posture, a slave of my own history? Am I to go on struggling until I am crushed into oblivion? Is there no more to life? Must I give it all I have just to build my shelter?

My life has been a chain of positions taken. I feel dragged down by it, tired of all my choices, exhausted by my own truths, mired in my successes. I made the effort to show a sunny face, climbed eagerly over all the opposing walls, piled sacks of sand... I am tired, ready to take my bow. Why isn't the curtain falling?

KNIGHT OF CLUBS

•

The Knight of Clubs is armed and shiny, as prepared as he will ever be. The day is bright, the air so clean. He can see no obstacle anywhere. Perhaps yonder in those distant mountains...

His horse, stout as it is, seems playful. The rider, his visor lifted, wears a perplexed look on his face and ponders whether he shouldn't rather dismount and use his weapons to till the fields and plant. No matter how much I ride, he thinks, I shall never reach the future.

The only thing to do is give his weapons and his labors to others. He can no longer ensure a safe passage for those who follow. His mastery will make his children no wiser, or their trails less treacherous. Danger cannot be balked. He knows nothing of the snares hungry for his children. He loves his children, but now they need to fend for themselves.

He wants no future, and will build no palace, for himself or for his, as those far mountains still beckon. The soil is ready for his seed. He sets aside the armor and readies for love.

•

Does anybody know where fear hides?

Life has left a vacuum in your heart; today you realize how long you've been trying to fill it.

To that end you became amiable, or else surly; your eyes sparkled with a smile, or else your face crumpled into a grimace. You wanted to appear jovial, sad. You played keen or mean, smart or stark.

Does it matter?

What or who is this wild horse you are spurring? And what are you going to do with the club in your hand?

QUEEN OF CLUBS

•

Oh, there are thorns on her all right, on my Black Rose... Yet her beauty is as overwhelming as her power. She walks tall, on her large feet, and her arms move about as in the dance of Kali, the transformer. Her hair sways as she moves her head in laughter, and her piercing dark eyes miss nothing as she moves about sorting, ordering, naming the plants by their Latin names. And she hoes the earth, and fertilizes the soil. And she sees in the apple blossoms of her groves the fruit they'll bear, and in the lilacs of her yard the perfume of her loving body.

Oh, my Black Rose of waiting, silken petals of my patience!

She waited fourteen years, count them: fourteen, for a kiss. And then that kiss had the moisture of the tears, the hunger of all the postponements, the ivory finish of the assured surrender of her lover. No fruit was ever riper, no bloom could hold more colors.

Oh my Black Rose of the ashes of time.

Nothing goes into the earth that will not be reborn as wood or fodder. And nothing ever loved as the flesh of my Black Rose.

•

In the late afternoon light, the dry weeds sizzle and shine. Is the day ending, or is the road? It's time for us to sit down, after a prayer, and look around and at those who go by. Let them forge ahead. Some go up, and some go down, but we forget the anxious trail we were following a few moments ago. We no longer know if we were coming closer or going away, ending or beginning. Let us pray, and be seated. For in sitting down we shall have the force of gravity—or of destiny, which is a form of gravity. Remember that the mountains in front of you have run just as much as the clouds now assaulting them.
Sit, and you shall reign.

Let us see the passage of others. Let us see the children that go into adulthood, and the adults that cannot go back to the child they were. And let us see how they all hurry.

Meanwhile there is blood raining on the hills.

KING OF CLUBS

•

His eyes have been trained to spot the weeds. His hand, offered to you in a sign of peace, has wielded the hoe and the sickle. The straightness of his regal back follows his many years of bending down to earth. His strength is always offered to the moment, for he knows the iris will burn inwards as it wilts, he knows that each spring pushes for summer, forever, and the sacred heaving of the seasons is the music we must all dance to.

So he may appear like a boor to you, callous and emotionless, immanently himself in the world, the sovereign of a self that cannot be explained. He is the King of Clubs, his scepter a pruning saw, his ermine a weathered flannel, his crown a sweaty bandanna. You might as well bend the oldest oak with your hands as sway this man.

•

The end of this spring—the withering broom blossom, and the bonfires on Saint John's eve—is a luminous triumph. Night has migrated to the other end of the earth, and none of us fear its return. We are strong. Out of luck and mere chance. A hit, a coincidence, the right time, a favorable wind, an idea, an inspiration. Let us not be proud of our efforts, even less of our merit. Let us rejoice for having been present at the happy windfall. No money in the world can buy the rain.

And this is our strength: pure accident.

Let us toss our coin into the air for heads or tails. And let us harbor no doubt: its answer will be what we need.

THE LESSER SECRETS

2

ACE OF CUPS

•

Your hand holds the goblet of your longings. It holds the water of mystery, the tears, the hopes, the apprehensions. These waters might appear as the lapping sounds of the waves on a deserted beach, at dawn, kissing the surrendering sand, or as a mountain lake, all splattered with water lilies that recede as the oars of your boat cut through and splash them with drops shinier than diamonds.

Unperceived until now, the water of your dreams has grown to fill the cup which, offered by your extended arm, becomes weighty as it loads the unforeseen and the unknown. How deep that water can be. How silent it is.

•

Do not be afraid of giving, now. With open hands. Some, near you, are thirsty. Let your liberality quench them. Your gift for them now is a true communion, and your offering, instead of making you superior and distant, will make you their equal. Their deserving or undeserving reception will bless you.

As you allow the others to drink from your cup, try not to tilt it, do not spill its contents, stir or shake them. As you give, now more than ever, you must keep your balance and stay within your line. Give them your drink, but not your soul.

TWO OF CUPS

•

Two is for alliance, and an alliance is always consecrated with a toast, the clinking of two cups. The two snakes are entwined around the caduceus, the mathematical formula revolves around the equal sign, the laced fingers of two friends bind their encounter as equals. For when we mate, we come to the common ground of humanity, and we forget both the exaltation of our pretensions, and the abasement of our fears: we are. And we drink to celebrate our being, our commonality, the magnificence of our humble state.

Let us therefore couple without pretense and without relinquishing. How majestic are the trees as they bow to the lashes of the storm, how luminous the cloud obeying the wind. Let us mate without relinquishing and without pretense. Let us not sell our soul for the contract with someone we think admirable. Let us not give up the journey of our self for the company of a parent surrogate. Let us not pretend and conquer the object of our ego's cravings. Let us not sell out to advantageousness. Let us love as truly as the rivers flow, and as mercilessly.

•

Now the two cups are empty. The union is no more. The libation has been consumed. The couple has been rent apart.

Oh, your tears may fill back your cup, but with how sour a potion! Alone now, you no longer can test your own humanity. Gone is your trusting, and something feels dead inside you. You must embark on a vessel of sorrow, a craft of selfishness, a shadowy eye of inner quest. Two empty cups!

You are left with the bitter thirst of your old mortality.

THREE OF CUPS

•

Some speak of a third eye of enlightenment and place it slightly above the level of the other two. And so your wisdom is on a different plane: above the norm, or below, it doesn't matter. The third eye sees things from an unreal perspective, but with a real feeling of serenity. You float outside of the common concern. The Greeks called this state *ataraxia* or un-murkiness; the Italians, *sprezzatura* or disinterest; some today speak of detachment, and the Buddha called it *nirvana*. Your third eye will never show on the bathroom mirror, will not come out in your pictures. You will be surprised by it, when your friend recognizes it and thanks you for its light. It was so natural, so easy... This, my wisdom? This normality?

Yes, your festive garland is obvious to all but you, appreciated like the trillium in the forest, like a trio of threes to the card player. You are Hermes the Thrice-greatest, crowned with trefoil like a silly old fool, triumphant in your self-oblivion. Tender thrashings of triple loves. You have climbed the steps to the threshold. Behold!

•

In three we make the train, and in threes the chain. Triple and tremendous is the trembling. Three is for a feast or for a treason. And three is the cipher of eternity.

Things could be long now, a tiresome tertian, a labyrinthine triangle, a trespass of tremendous consequences, a trip, or a tripping, or a trap.

Your melody will be in the treble clef.

But do not light three on a match.

FOUR OF CUPS

•

A man is contemplating his failures. Are they three, are they thirty? Yet he has managed to preserve his—shall we say innocence? He has maintained a kind of youthfulness, but also a kind of loneliness. It has brought him unscathed to this safe place and momentary repose. He sits atop a hillock, shaded by a lone tree, and considers the three cups he has drunk to the dregs. Now his angel of reality brings him a fourth cup.

The man takes the cup and brings it to his heart. Then he lowers his lips to the lip of the fourth cup, contemplates his own reflection on the liquid, and drinks. The angel quickly, too quickly, is gone.

The man places the cup alongside the other three. They are all full again, and he prays for thirst.

•

In the Romance languages one does not waste time but loses it. This Four of Cups is an unambiguous card that tells you to go and lose time; shake off the old tick-tock that has been tailing you. Lose yourself into any completely gratuitous activity. Take a walk, a nap. Or sit on a chair and stare at the wall. Be welcoming at the door to which no one comes.

And so that you do not waste time before you start to lose time, this card now says no more.

FIVE OF CUPS

•

Three down, and two to go. You have drunk up the milk from three of the five goblets you were allotted—for this adventure or for this life. Two of them tasted sweet, the third tasted bitter.

You are brooding over these three chalices and ignoring the other two. The grayness of the sky makes you believe the sun is gone for good. The gurgling of the water—you must soon cross, the river distracts you from finding the bridge.

You stand with bowed head. Impatience will surely tempt you. If you give in to it, you'll disregard the fact that the decision to fill the remaining chalices is yours and only yours. You will obsess about the liquid you consumed, and spilled, instead of opening towards the future and freeing your potential.

•

And then we die.

One: My friend the poet has me read his sonnet translating a dead poet's sonnet about his blindness.

Two: My friend the jilted lover pours her anger onto me, like a wave, frothing.

Three: My dead mother now holds back her love, now sends forth her kindness. Oh, mother, pray for me.

Four: I busy myself at planning, and hoping, and working. I am lost in the folds of my living shroud, and I want to build my fortress.

Five: Our tears and our laughter help us join together in our only respite against the wake, our oblivion.

Oh, murderous life. The cup of those who cannot forget holds only poison.

SIX OF CUPS

•

If you want the world to be large again, cleared of deceit and of mediocrity, a place where wonder plays like sunshine on the waves, a place for awe and greatness, and with a path marked for your passing alone, you must become a child again.

You must again undo the hard lessons of experience, the rules of expeditiousness to which you have trained your brain. Again a child! Grow small and listen to your passion. Take the advice of your elders as if it were a story you heard by the hearth. Fill your six cups with earth, as you did with sand to build the castles of your seashore fantasies, then plant the seeds of your future.

Remember that innocence is the best fertilizer.

•

What lies upriver, in the heart of darkness? How come the waters of the rivers, coming from the small, keep flowing without drying up? The journey, like any journey, is a pilgrimage to the source; upstream lies a paradise, like all paradises, lost. As you prepare your ascent, cleanse the six goblets of your adulthood: fear and comfort, impatience and boredom, pride and despair.

Now is the time to abandon your boat.

You may take along only what will fit in your knapsack. You are allowed only six questions. Choose them well, for the trek is long.

SEVEN OF CUPS

•

There are many recipes for sleep. Just yesterday I read one in an ancient volume. The potion recommended was made of a mixture of frog's spittle, morning dew from the leaves of the mandrake, and peacock's urine, to be stirred together with the knucklebone of a stillborn seventh son. Today, when I looked for it again to learn the exact proportions, I could not find it, even though I had made a note of page and tome. Did I perhaps dream it?

Sleep is difficult. In the past, I had forgotten how to sleep, and then learnt it anew. But perhaps I should first learn how to dream. Dreams come, and persist or puff away, always beyond the control of our minds. And this is the card of the seven wonders of my secret self-dreams of love and of mystery, of fears and glory, of cruelty and riches, and the movable landscapes of the soul—revealed to me by my dream, existing as the iridescence on the tender skin of black hot pitch.

•

Seven are the days of the week, and seven the locks on the tomb that must never be opened. Seven is the number of play and complication, and the sign on the plateau of your attainment: do not forget what you are for the sake of getting what you want.

For wanting is not like hunger that can be satisfied. Wanting is a gift; it will elevate you when you do not tame it, when you let it be inside you like pure air in your lungs. And wanting will poison you when you pump your desire with the foul gases of your calculation. Lead your life, not your biography.

Let your dreams guide you, but let them be pure. Let go of your image. Stop endeavoring to appear, in the eyes of others, solid as a rock or frail as a wounded bird. Give up the struggle to become what you are not meant to be. Save the effort for another moment. Breathe!

EIGHT OF CUPS

•

Scabrous as your past may be, ignoring it is always an act of desperation. For you cannot overcome anything you do not own or divorce anyone you haven't married; and parting without a goodbye will sour your blood. The Eight of Cups is the card of a mid-way crisis; it tells you to look forward and back, lest you walk into darkness.

Can you make a list with the eight components of what has fed you until now? The cool potion of your love, the hot brew of your desire, the chewy oatmeal of your will, the crusty bread of your work, the clear broth of your learning, the sweet custard of your play, the gruff gumbo of your patience, the spice liquor of your friendship—they have all left traces inside your cups. Clean them before you leave and set your cups in order. As much as you can. Human affairs will never attain an absolute order.

•

How will my face look in the mirror of eternity? How old shall I be in heaven—or hell? How old are my dead parents now? And what is the age of the unborn? The heat of Hades is tempered by the waters of Lethe.

We can only think of loss as walking away. And we feel bad, as if we had left those who have died, as if it had been us walking away from them. For indeed now we have to face our road alone, weighed down by memories and distress, under the mocking light of the moon for whom all change is futile. While we are mired in change, and take pride in our mortality, we can feel our minds swell with their illusions of permanence. Others die, we think, they pass away; we forget that the world is a jumble of velocities, and beauty but oblivion. How long does a firefly live?

NINE OF CUPS

•

The augury is definitely one of satisfaction. You see how simple it is to enjoy what you have, once you stop choking it with your grip. Nothing much to it: you say what you think, enjoy what you have. Forget the weather forecast and don't begrudge the rain, or the heat. And most of all, resist all temptations of saving, for saving will insure your poverty and bastardize your joy. Make your present the antechamber to a chimera.

Don't even count your blessings; let them be. Why rush to be early somewhere else when you are here now? And do not ask yourself if you are happy; happiness is nothing more than the past of a present lived well.

After all, where else would you want to be? Is there any place without sunsets? Here you are now in the place that has chosen you with all the weight of history.

•

I see a man. He looks wealthy; he has dark hair and is rather pudgy: his table is well-provided. This man could have a great influence on your life. Not necessarily a bad influence. It could be a beneficial influence, but with some touches of discomfort.

Here we have, in truth, abundance. An abundance that cost some effort. The table with the nine cups is disproportionately tall, not easily reached. It is provided for a feast, but one can never ensure that the celebration will proceed smoothly. Abundance creates complication.

PAGE OF CUPS

•

How can you forget your deeds and not take them to bed with you? No one sleeps more soundly than the child in the care of the family, or the slave who has lost the taste for freedom. But being you, how can you attain your rest?

Take your work and leave it at the door of someone to care for it. Offer it cleanly and happily. Say the magic word: enough!

As for the rest... Think the world is never in order. The weeds push through, autumn will follow summer, and the ones you love trudge along wanting what they want and erring as they will. That day in which everything will be orderly and under control—no beds to make, no bills to pay, no apologies to offer, no drudgery to face—will never come. We might as well pretend today is that day.

•

Sexual impulse is always a surprise, an unexpected sighting of a doe. No maps, no field glasses were needed.

Desire is a passing thing, the happy encounter of the moment, the playfulness of unpremeditation. Go slow, when you sense it, go slow. Speak your desire plainly and clearly, and do not make a big thing of it—that would only get you into a mess. The gods grant us desire when they know we need it—and then some. So, it is better to waste it than to turn it into the brainy subject of strategy. Let us not hide our desire in the recondite folds of our resolve.

This card, then, warns us not to take our sexual impulse too seriously, not to make it an excuse for self-blame, or self-pity, even less to force ourselves upon some innocent. We have the capacity—of such breed are the powers we've been granted—to rot the gods' good gifts into poison.

KNIGHT OF CUPS

•

Now is the time for cleaning house, for going out into the open air, for making decisions. Now is the time to remember your own center and strength, to walk straight and upright. Remember: what the others say is their affair. Now more than ever. Don't let words born perhaps of envy, even malice, distract you from listening to your own heart.

You are clean, prepared, and advancing, whether you know it or not. You yourself are the message of peace and health, and you are one with the universe just as the message is one with the messenger. It is because you see that the sky is blue. The water is transparent for your eyes. Your horse obeys your signals.

When you answer with a pure heart the question "Who am I?" you will see yourself with the resplendence of your beauty. Do not despair if the hardships of the road you now follow are the only reminder of your strength, or if your tiredness is the only thing that speaks to you of your glory in the world.

•

Do not let your weapons make you forget your offering.

You will never regret having done good. As you try on your plate armor, make sure it doesn't encumber the movement of your hand as it offers a teeming cup.

Watch out, though. Many will knock on your door. If you defer to the will of all, you might miss the road that's best. They will knock on your door and beg. They will implore, with cries and smiles, sparing no tricks, in a thousand tongues. Beg they will, and not always for their own good. Or yours.

If you now encounter the one who recites to you a list of needs, and pleads with you to fulfill them, remember you are armed and stand in the midst of a region not always open nor clear.

Giving is not conceding. Be mindful of your self!

KING OF CUPS

•

Just as the summer is coming to an end, the possessions of this world will also come to an end. Everything, however, must first reach its culmination, and we must rejoice in it before we let go of it forever. This is a moment of culmination gathering in its plenitude all that has been developing during the last twelve weeks.

Behind you are your travels and perils; of the tempestuous waters which you have navigated all that's left now is a small sample filling your cup.

The moment is one of safety and solemnity. The monster you came face to face with is now drowned in the waters of time. But the golden fish hanging from the chain you wear around your neck reminds you that, as all endings are also beginnings, a new cycle is about to start.

You hold in your cup the liquid of your experience. You may rightly feel serene, calm and in control of the situation. For how long? Ah, but the sovereignty implies the dismissal of time. Don't beckon the future. Reign.

•

The upside-down of the card, however, fills with presages. They are subtle presages, and nothing may ever come of them. And it may be better not to see them come true, for things move at an unavoidable pace, always beyond our control. The water that fills your cup is the sea that has brought you away from the others.

Perhaps the best way to mediate on the King of Cups is with a somewhat philosophical vision:

Triumph and dominion are tantamount to loneliness; only in humiliation you can find true company—in making yourself humble, human, close to the earth's humus. Only in letting go can you find true power. If the experience that enriched you brought you to isolation, your sovereignty—your voice now your own and not an echo of your chimera's—will take you back to your people. Hold lightly to your power and to the indissolubility of your self. Accept your full being like you accept your shadow.

QUEEN OF CUPS

•

A little wine in the goblet will suffice for us to know what our wealth is. Reaching the shore's sand may be all the travel we need. Sitting just a spell will give us the necessary rest. After the shroud of clouds breaks, the earth quenched by rain, the sky returns to the serenity that is its law.

Keep in your goblet a little—even if only a few drops—of the best of your loving. Do not pour all of your love into it for you would become dry. Place just a few drops in the goblet, and then close the lid on them, and let the vase rest.

When the feeling of longing hits you do not open the cup yet. Look at it for a while: closed, shining, wise, sacred.

•

Who is this woman who won't look at me, and what does she hold in her cup? She sits in splendor facing the waters—the waters of inebriation and oblivion, eddying playfully, their surface echoing with a naiad's sighs. Is she perhaps the old Provençal N'Oc-e-No, Ms. Yes-and-No, known to poets then, and resurfaced now for the continued puzzlement of the thirsty?

Impossible to tell anything about her. She's evasive; her gaze wanders. She will talk to me—words, words—but will not look at me. Her face in three-quarter profile, her eyes floating away... to Byzantium?

Who is she, and what does she want? And what does the cup hold? Is she offering it to me? Is she bemoaning its emptiness? Is all this the naiad's fantasy swirling in the water, kissing its surface like a drowned dragonfly? Is this just my own reflection on the water, the mirror or my drained heart? Or the mist of my fantasies, the promises born of my yearnings, the mirage of my doom, the figuration of my death?

THE LESSER SECRETS

3

ACE OF SWORDS

•

You will feel the piercing and then the gash—when you least expect it. You were feeling content and, all of a sudden, your flesh is rent, and you come to see that all you had built is but the veil of an illusion now being ripped.

But how painful is the cut? The feeling is acute, deep, cleaving, but you are hurt more by its abruptness than by its harm—as indeed there is something sovereign about the blow, something cleansing about the surprise, something strengthening about the experience.

What is all this about? It could be the coming to its end of an intimate relationship. (At first, you'll feel attacked in your integrity and your effectiveness.) It could be the ending of a project or a job. (At first, you'll feel left out in the cold, betrayed.) You are again facing conflict. Whatever it is, the change is undeniable, and there is no going back. Transformation has begun. These are other times. Even the weather is different now. The air is colder (cleaner, too) and the moment offers you the chance to grab your sword and reclaim your fullness and your integrity, the kingdom of your self.

You are again facing conflict, but this time you do not need to resort to ruses of self-denial because now you hold the sword of your own strength.

•

The pain tells you that you have come into contact with your doom. Not only are you your own enemy, but your strength has misshapen and fated your life. Not all your strength, but one of the strengths you hold sovereign: your critical powers. You have been able to deflate everybody's arguments, including your own. You have compared, and judged, and answered any question with incisive aftersight. Needs editing, you've said. That will never sell, you've prognosticated. Not as good as..., you've indicated. You have made all the fine arguments, pointed out everything notable, redressed all typos, crossed all t's and dotted all i's. Your mediocrity looms now like a scarecrow all dressed up in silks and moirés and ostrich feathers.

But the sword of your wit has also turned against you, and against the center of your being: your passion. Isn't this the familiar voice: "Why bother to write if no publisher will want to print my book? Why bother to practice if no concert hall will hear my music? Why paint if no gallery will exhibit my picture?"

So, triumphant with your premonition of failure, you have ceded your waking hours to calculation, sacrificed your bliss to ambition, and enslaved your soul to the tasks that bear no risk.

TWO OF SWORDS

•

We carry our strength with ease, with surprising ease, and yet we are blind to it. Our fortitude often stems from two different, even contrary forces. In the equilibrium between those contrary forces lies peace. Whenever we favor one potency no more than the other we find calm, the sedate and stable sensation of our nature. From two evils balanced against each other may come one good. Perhaps the solution to a problem goes by way of another problem.

Let us not dwell in our defects, for greater folks than us have been granted worse natures. Let us not get stuck trying to eradicate those flaws our minds are ready to condemn; let us rather look for a compensating virtue and let it grow in us—so that the lazy shall look for strength, the angry for prudence, and the desperate shall turn their gaze to the Star. Blaming our thirst is not the same as seeking water.

Two are the swords in the compass that will trace the regular and perfect circle, the mathematical path, the precise itinerary that always reverts upon itself.

•

But now you feel an equilibrium of forces that is also an uproar. Appearances have become fallacious. You feel frenzied as your head fusses with them. Lies, deceit, and even treason, swarm in the air you breathe. The horizon blurs and disappears and a confusion arises out of the sky and sea, islands and clouds.

Inaction is the underside of equilibrium. Pray for hope whenever you cannot tell apart envy and desire. Keep in mind that the night is just beginning and that it would be folly not to expect the light of morning.

THREE OF SWORDS

•

Three swords pierce your heart. Their cuts are deep, unequivocal.

One sword is the pain of absence. The person we love is far, and our loneliness hurts. It hurts even more as we suspect we had something to do with its arrival, that we have somehow provoked it.

The second is the sword of honesty, of the pain that forces us to recognize our limits. It is the inarguable cut reminding us that we can never become aware of our own virtue, that whenever we do a good deed we do so by the grace that lets us participate in the good already existing in the world. This is the sword to remind us we are only a part of the world and of life.

The third sword is that of treason, of any treason perpetrated on us. This sword reminds us that the pain we feel—whether we attribute it to our enemies, to our problems, to the devil, to our error—is authentic and real, and not the vagaries of our fantasy.

•

Darkness comes a few minutes earlier as days grow short now. With the impatience of modern idolatry, having made a fetish of my control over things, I hasten to deny the onset of night. Before the light begins to fade I rush to turn on my lamps.

With darkness outside and the lights on in my room, as I look out the window, I see my own reflection. The glass pane gives me back my bed, deformed by my nightly habituation. Half-read books lie on the bedside table; perhaps I shall never finish reading them, even though in the light of my mirror I think myself immortal.

If I waited to turn on the lights, if I accepted the dark and protested my mortality less, then through the window I would see the stars.

FOUR OF SWORDS

•

The devil comes and tells us we are dust, and that to dust we are to return. Yes, it's the devil; you can be sure of that. The angels would rather tell us we are earth: from the earth we are born, and from the earth we feed, and to the earth we shall return. We are, even in death, fertile earth rather than sterile dust.

The Romans called the fecund dirt *humus*, and we, following their words, exhume secrets, and inhume the dead. This earth is what makes us human.

Earth is one of our four strengths. And to accept that strength we need a virtue that is hard to learn: humility, the consciousness of being earth and dirt, *humus*, a bunch of molecules roaming the surface of the planet, a mutability pining for repose.

And so we face our need for humility as we now enter this period of work without recompense, of hard-earned seclusion, this time to cement our selves, without clear results, without even thoughts of results—other than that ultimate and much-feared humbleness. But need we fear it?

Let our feet be planted on the ground; may our obstinate and earthy work continue. Let our thoughts of gilded death be the fallow for our souls.

•

Mediocrity is pushed along by envy and pride, the opposites of humility. Envy is a potent potion, it moves mountains; pride is even stronger.

But what shall we do? We all hold indeterminate quantities—some more, some less—of envy and pride, even the false pride that makes us think that our luck, our fluky luck, is the mark of our superiority. Many of our undertakings have been fueled by these dark, rocky qualities. Their workings have the weightiness of will; but will is a moisture-thirsty mortar, prone to crack and crumble.

The four swords, the weight of metal, the balance of opposites, the regulation of life, the calculation of effort... Shall we convert our lives into our résumés? Shall we make ourselves into our own mausoleum? Our image on the tomb looks noble, solid and lasting; as statues, we look dignified and handsome. My, oh my, won't the children who see us be frightened!

FIVE OF SWORDS

•

Let them moan and weep, and let them give up the struggle. They have their reasons, and they feel the power of those reasons. Now, you take up arms and get ready, for the battle draws near.

Very little is known about this battle. Nothing, really. We only know what it isn't. For it has nothing to do with our heads, with our ideas, or our reasoning. It has nothing to do with expectations and decisions. Something, perhaps, with our teeth and guts. The explanations are to come later, much later. And they will be bursting with the wisdom of belatedness.

This moment has some sprinklings of folly. You need all your folly to face the giants, the ghouls and spooks, the gummed-hair Draculas. You must take action. But what action? Can you find enemies to smite that are not already within you?

•

The signs are hard to read. The pitch of confusion sticks to our syllables and to our breath. Things aren't going the way they should; our vision dims in somberness. Days swirl into mazes. Opinions diverge. The clouds in the sky draw erratic calligraphies. Everything is ciphered in unreal omegas.

There is a stench in the air. The sufferings of the world appear in our neighborhood. We smell death. We sense treason.

But we can only advance towards cold and darkness, even though all the clothes we have are old. Our friends went into hiding; those who love us are far. Doors are banging from a gust of wind.

SIX OF SWORDS

•

This is the time of passage and of decision, and so you will decide and shed, just as the deciduous trees all around you decide and let go of their leaves, blood and gold to the ground. Six—the half dozen—marks the middle of the way, just as the Hallows' day stands between the equinox and the solstice.

This is the time for planning and reflecting, and for turning your gaze Janus-like to the past and to the future. Signs are bound to appear also with double meanings, and they will be hard to read, even to identify. Yet we must make decisions and stick to them. Hesitation is deadly.

Here is one sign: a sad but courageous woman will appear on your path. This attractive woman will be sitting by the side of the road. You must stop to talk to her, and she will tell you her story. It would be an error, however, to intervene. Let her go, wherever she is headed, do not attach yourself to her beyond your attentive conversation. Hear her and bless her and let her go. But remember her story and heed her words for you.

•

Your boat separates the waters. As you cross the river, which is untiring, you have murky waters to one side, placid waters to the other. On your boat, which is small, sit your people, who are few. Impaled on a bench are the six swords of past sufferings.

You don't know what awaits you on the opposite shore. You suspect it is much like the one you have left. Yet, when you get there, you will find that the river of bloody waters and its difficult portage have changed you. Once on that shore you can abandon this boat pierced by the six swords of your sorrows.

SEVEN OF SWORDS

•

This feeble and yellow light saturates everything and plays upon your masks. The short daylight and the lowered beams make you appear different and diverse, with as many lives as a cat, wild and messy, fussy and defiant, purring and pouncing in turns.

The war has come to a halt. The stability of its contenders was too great. We had set our camp with the anticipation of an easy victory, but we are now beginning to see that the siege had become habit, that we have been routed by rote, our energy turned to inertia. We could go on, and spend a whole lifetime of war, a war with causes that fade into dry oblivion.

We had everything so well prepared... All too well. We planted our swords on the ground right next to our tents, so as to have them ready at hand, and so as to be able to engage in battle at the first bugle call.

But a fool came, unexpected as are all fools, and stole all the swords. We are sitting in council, just a few yards away; our plans were so clever... Now, what?

•

I must face a transition. I must assume a new reality, retreat back to my life before the seven swords of my disappointments. I must regain the sense of novelty that set me on my path. Think of my career, even before it was a good idea, or an idea at all, when it was all passion. See if I can recover that moment of wonder and lightness, when for the first time I tried my hand at what is now my job. I felt indifferent to it all then, cared little about any results that might ensue, thought little of an audience or a master or the customers. Can I now go back to that pure me, pure trying, pure unexpectancy?

It is time to return to that selfless origin, to see how interesting disinterestedness makes everything. To let the swords go—my weapons and my trials—and be. Even at the height of my battle, I can surrender into just being.

EIGHT OF SWORDS

•

Eight demons follow you. One is the demon of fear, fear that gnaws the inside of your throat. Two is the demon of doubt, the faithlessness that simmers in your brain. Three is the demon of distorted memories, thoughts that remake the past in the light of lies. Four is the demon of feigned love, or the unwanted sex of conquests and surrender. Five is the demon of haste that hurries you away to where no one is calling. Six is the demon of false virtue, the offspring of ambition and delusion, the parent of bitter gifts and rotten sacrifices. Seven is the demon of the yoke of grudges you drag wherever you go. And Eight is the infinite demon of lists and accounts, the greed of immaterial mathematics.

Sharpen your eight swords.

•

Then we don't know what to do, what road to take, what answers to give. We feel gagged; all we can tell is that we are treading a ground made slippery with brackish waters, and that somewhere near rises the castle of our dreams. Fear has disguised itself as lethargy, shame is the pall that darkens the sky, envy has killed all wind; a false hope makes us long for a liberator we do not need.

Yes, sometimes we are distracted.

Sometimes we are imprudent.

Discipline fails us often.

And there is the weather, the storms that affect us: fatigue and disillusion, dismay and even despair. Yes, the weather.

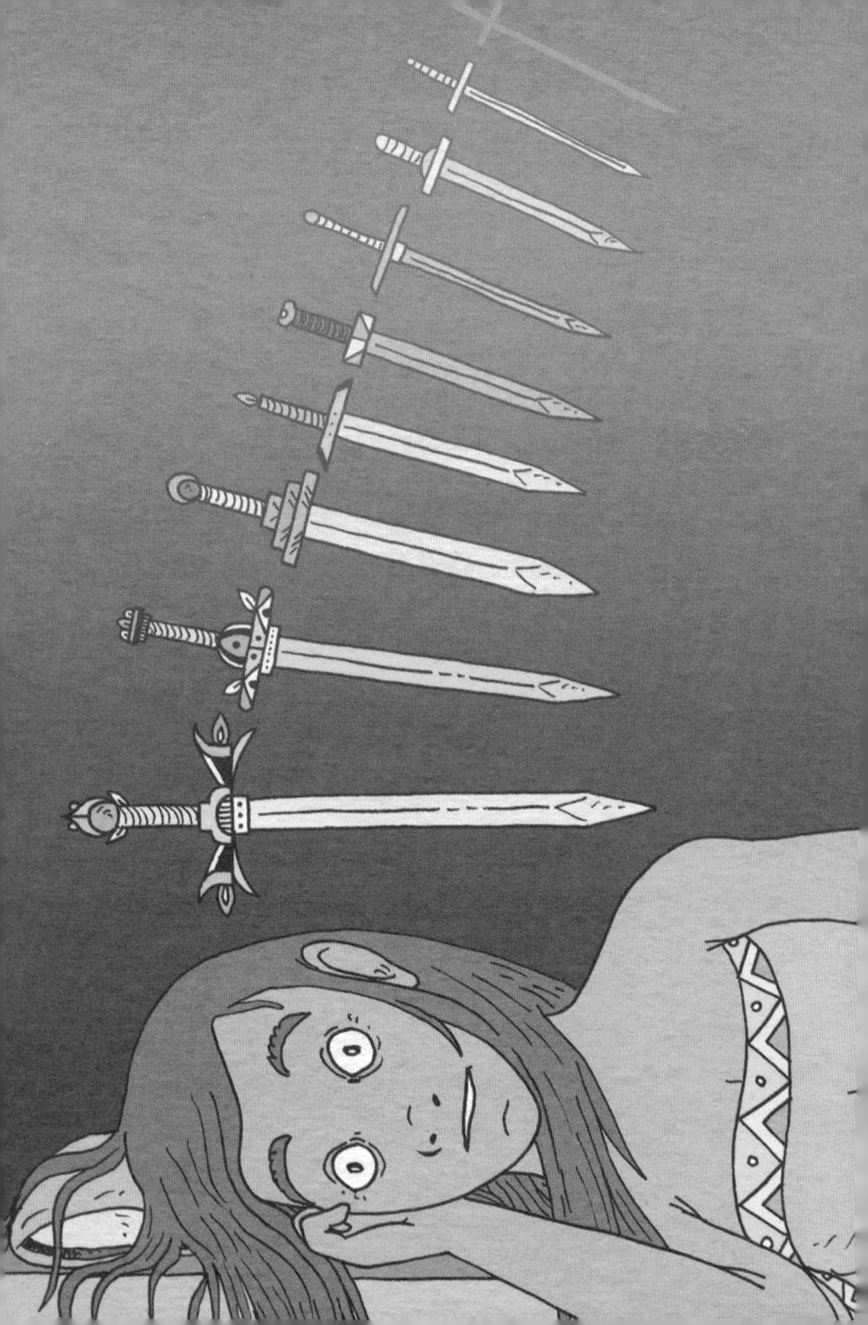

NINE OF SWORDS

•

The night is cold, but you have a bed of roses.

Many are the difficulties of hard times; and they multiply themselves to the threshold of infinity as symbolized by the number nine. Do not waste your sleep debating your troubles.

The night is fierce, but you have a bed of roses.

The experience you have accumulated gives you the strength of nine swords, but it can also weigh grievous on your mind. Your very might may be your fright.

The night is cruel, but you have a bed of roses.

You cannot make the past go away by covering your eyes; you cannot grow your nails long enough to scour your shame.

The night is deadly, but you have a bed of roses.

•

Beware of the nine swords of your nightmares. They will pin your life against the sands of your rue if you first do not rise to own them. Those piercing voices of your darkest dreams, make them yours; see what fears feed them, what their parents are, and their children. Turn your other cheek, for only this will disarm them—and if they ask you to go one mile with their burden, offer to go two miles. Do not oppose your pride to their pride.

Do not fatigue your fate. You have already sought too many signs. You have prepared too much and now your armor drags you down. You have consulted too many oracles and addressed too many gods. You have encumbered advisors and friends. The time has come to try something new.

Undo your fists into receiving hands.

PAGE OF SWORDS

•

Why forgo the exhilaration of the road, renounce our freedom, refuse the invitation of a breeze? It is time to lose the heaviness of nightmares stuffed with doubts, harbingers of husky decisions and incisive examinations. The door is no longer locked.

This Page is coming out of the chamber that made everything dark and attracted the fears of long-drawn nights. She is now at the point of tasting her liberation, her escape into bliss, the lightness of the road gently rolling under the boots of her new dreams. Her past will remain in the chamber; the airs of now will cleanse her chest. The sword she holds is the sword of competence; her competence is born of acceptance. Nothing could be easier. Wisdom and love lie ahead.

•

You must lose yourself before you find yourself. Surrender to your darkness. Rescue the raw sorrows of your childhood; weep them afresh with grown-up tears. We must be human, all too human, before we melt into the divine. Passion precedes Glory. Let your life come back to you like a wave born of the undertow. Remember all things must pass.

The pain shall pass, and the new-found folly. And the glory to come later shall pass. And so will the soothing consolation given us by the knowledge that all shall pass.

If your worry doesn't let you see those birds taking flight, take a leap into the now. Stop your steps, turn your head backwards, hold your balance, breathe, and say: I am.

Or, if you wonder whether this journey is really your journey, let the question be; for perhaps that question, for all its anguish, is what makes the moment yours. One thing you will always be allowed to know: that you are, that you are yourself. Only pure hope will never abandon you. Keep your sword; do not exchange it for someone else's tempting baggage.

KNIGHT OF SWORDS

•

You mounted the horse of useless preparation. Which by extension means, just about, that the most sublime moments of happiness often spring from something simple, unforeseen. And victory from defeat.

At the strike of the hour, you donned your coat of mail and your armor over it, topped your head with a plumed helmet, and draped it all with the cloths stamped with the emblem of your Lady and of your cause.

And so you mounted your nag and spurred him on. And down you go, racing the wind, grabbing your unsheathed sword for the blow against the enemy.

But where's the enemy? Or who is it? Is it a windmill or a flock of sheep to make a Fool out of you? Or is it the enchanter who had robbed you of your worth?

But it matters little because today's attack will lend its sense to tomorrow's forgiveness.

•

Plans, calculations, and brainy decisions are not always the causes of our successes. Our best moves come from an unreasoned center in our body, spontaneously as it would seem. As we realize this, we then pay implicit homage to reason and to judgment.

Let us not dismiss all the thinking that seemed for naught, the preparation for stillborn projects, the plans doomed to yellow on the paper. Without our dead-end paths, our horizons would shrink under the waves of the slightest storm. We cannot prepare spontaneity. A sudden intuition, the just response issuing from our gut, the rush of genius—or its glimpse—are all related to our prudence.

Need we despair? Need we sheath our sword? But let us not grab it so firmly either, let it be one with our arm. Let the wind be one with our face and clothing, and our wrath be one with our pardon.

QUEEN OF SWORDS

•

Give up and give in and set your mind free.

Then you shall reign. You will soar with the butterfly wings of angels, and the clouds will pay homage at your feet, monarch of the air and of the sky.

Your solitude is your triumph over loneliness. Against the feeling of dejection, let us oppose that of sovereignty. For truly there is something sovereign in solitude, and something solitary in sovereignty.

Alone and majestic, the Queen of Swords admonishes and forgives, she understands as she judges, while she at once pleases and imposes.

She sits above clouds and storms, and way behind her lie the hardships of the road she followed among blackened trees and craggy rocks. A lone hawk soars against the blue.

•

And this Queen used to be a spoiled brat, the Princess. She needed homage from others because she could not get her own. She needed to think she was better in order to feel she was any good. And so she bitched and pleaded and was sad in her heart every time someone she knew had a little triumph. For she needed to feel she was better in order to think she was any good.

What made her change? What freed her from her pupa of loneliness and released the wings of her self? Even though infected by the silk of her cage, she was aching for her self. She wanted to be free at last from the enslavement of her ego, that conglomerate of fear and bruised experience held together by the chains of causality. Free from the dogs of self-pity, from the strings of rote and the nets of duty.

So she stopped pushing. She stopped defending her space. "You can't come in here," she had used to say; "if you do this, you'll pay for it! You're gonna get it this time! These are my limits, don't tread on me. Get out of my face! I won't have any of this!"

One day, as if touched by a magic wand, she tried to learn where her balance was, and concentrated on staying on her feet, rather than in her place; rather than having; on moving, rather than preventing the pushes from others. And it worked. And so here she is now, free to speak out and speak up, to do or rest, to fly or nest. The Queen of Swords.

And this is, oh patient reader, the moral of the story.

KING OF SWORDS

•

Nothing makes sense without love. There is no truth without love, and no love without truth. Easy shoulders to cry on are not love, nor is pity or compassion.

There is no passion and no freedom without love. The majesty of love will tell me who I am, from the crown of my glory to the roots of my sins; only love will see those connected, crown and root feeding each other for the tree. And the humbleness of love will help me accept the portrait presented to me. I learn only when I hitch my imagination to love.

The strength of the King of Swords is in his purity, in the naked sword of his truth. The sword is his weapon and the symbol of the sovereignty he has earned. But his sword, as much as his innocence, cuts and slashes. My ego will hurt and my image will crumble, but only the King's sword can raise me to the nobility of my self.

My strength is my serenity, my temper. I must let go, both of empty exaltations and fatiguing fears. My strength is my acceptance. I must receive the might of the earth and of roots; a strength without eyes and without memory. A pure rock, open to the world, edgier than any illusion.

•

It is not difficult to see the deceit behind the throne. The upside down of this card comes to caution you:

For you may be deceived by a serene countenance, a noble stance, the loftiness of royal robes.

You may be deceived by a sharpened rectitude.

And you can also deceive yourself adopting airs of sober modesty while you wallow in your pride and envy. You can deceive yourself and, worse yet, you can deceive others—which will confirm your self-deceit, as deceit clones itself in its own echoes.

Do not drape your lies in the ermines of hypocrisy or vanity. Say nothing if it isn't the truth. Rejoice in nothing but the whole truth. You can only reign with those you love, and only love yourself in fullness. The rest is tyranny, or flattery.

THE LESSER SECRETS

4

ACE OF GOLDS

•

All is dark around you, all black. Allow your eyes to become used to the darkness. All is silent. All asleep. You feel alone in the world surrounded by the silence of death, immersed in non-occurrence.

Let your eyes become used to the darkness. Minutes will go by, half an hour, the whole night. A black velvet shrouds everything. There is nothing you can do.

Then, quietly, above you, a point of light.

It flickers like an unrecognized yearning. It's a star. A distant, solitary star. It takes body, little by little. Gradually, everything near you fills with its golden light. The warmth of its presence cleaves the pervading coldness. A sun star—golden, warm, resplendent. A perennial crown of ancient light. God's messenger. A friend of time.

•

Now consider the following vision:

The old man, laughing, lifts the girl in his arms. They look at each other and recognize each other. The old man sees in the soft rosiness of the girl and in her golden curls a reflection of his own past, of the youthful body he used to inhabit. The girl recognizes in the old man a twilight, a pathway ahead: the unavoidable passage of time, the imperfect ellipse of her own destiny. With cheeks fired up, by youth or by wine, the old man and the girl kiss and laugh.

This is the parable of beginnings, for even in old age there can be a new season, and an old man can again turn green like an apple bough in spring, though he is entering his winter years.

One thing we can do in this new season is get the critic inside each one of us drunk with the tiger's milk of laughter and love and detachment, free ourselves from ungodly ambition, and watch our criticism be diluted in that tiger's milk. So with renewed heart we set out on our journey toward spiritual awareness and toward joy.

TWO OF GOLDS

•

Someone offers us two closed fists. For which one shall we opt? The chosen hand turns over and opens slowly; one by one, its fingers stretch. But in the hand there is nothing, the nothingness of disillusion.

We must decide. We must resolve. We must act. It's not all gold that glitters. One of these two coins could be counterfeit. The moment for judgment has come; the moment for assessment, for knowledge. We must be careful.

Careful... things deceive. Whom shall we believe, the actor or the mask? Which one lies to us less?

The year begins for us. We are undertaking a new adventure. Let us enter this phase with care, with prudence.

•

You're lucky. Everything is going your way. Your egg had a double yolk. Your offspring will be twins.

Everything opens. Everything splits open—everything doubles over duplicitously. Even your inner self feels divided. Don't panic. Let yourself go. Let your trustiness show you that nothing matters, that your problems will solve themselves. Life is a gamble. And you're on a roll. It's so easy to win, to double your money. Play on. Double. Double or nothing...

Will the project that so worries you now ever come to fruition? It will, yes, thanks to your effort, but not thanks to your worrying; your worrying will not move it an inch closer to its completion. But are you sure you can tell your effort and your worrying apart? Is a will mired in your projected image really different from a vainglorious and compliment-seeking fretting?

The sun is rising but the darkness has not been dispelled.

THREE OF GOLDS

•

We shall start before the first rays of the sun, almost in darkness, and feel the cold under our stiff woolen coats. We shall strain our eyes to make out the plans, but we'll mix with a sure trowel the lime, sand, and water of the mortar.

We shall also address a prayer to the gods so that our muscles, our brain, and our soul work in good harmony. Also, three are the virtues we must pray for: Faith, the virtue of accepting the obvious; Hope, the virtue of rejecting the ruses that disguise the present as future; and Love, the virtue of letting others be, neither greater nor lesser than yourself. Let us pray for them with no demands; the gods adjust poorly to timetables.

We've set out on our road, even though we were shaking with cold and fear. We know we're emerging from the darkness and that the sun will rise, without our rushing—certainly without our rushing. Let us not forget that now is the time for action.

•

What a lazy day! It wasn't easy to get up. Took my time cuddling in the covers, wishing it were a holiday.

Found a thousand excuses to complicate things. Gossiped with my neighbor and, at work, it's been a constant argument. I thought it was white, my colleague thought it was black. Had an argument. Ended up disagreeing with my colleague, even though we were both probably saying the same thing. Almost came to blows.

The day went by fast, but, because I'd been feeling stubborn, it put me in an uneasy mood. What have I done to deserve this, I asked. Damn, oh, damn!

(As a prayer, or as a penance, imagine that your curse is an offering and take it to the temple of what you consider most holy.)

FOUR OF GOLDS

•

You could hold, you could grasp, you could sit tight with your teeth clenched. You could sulk, stuck onto your pride and your possessions, and turn your back to the work of others. You could believe you're the only one to ever have *made*. You could make yourself a frozen sculpture: no fear but no joy, no doubt but no discovery, no setbacks but no passion.

But let go of things and you'll see how each finds its counterbalance. Your heart is a flower, fragrant even as it droops, beautiful even as it wilts. All things have a point of compensation. Ambition could remain here, in equilibrium, in its allotted house. Everything to its place. Give the Caesar what is Caesar's...

You have enough, really. And you have done enough. Everything is the way it should be. The beam of sun filtering through your window is all the light you need. If you could only see the world's unrelenting change. But you cannot see change because, before all change, this arctic Now lies mired in its wish to overcome the inevitable. Our effort breaks down within the heartbeat of the universe.

•

Work is not everything. When well planned, it leaves a space in its middle. The four gold coins that form the basis of your effort move to the corners. In that center some new symbols appear. What do they say? They are hard to read.

A journey is now offered to you. Is it an actual journey, or is it the mercurial instability of the universe? Hard to tell. They will not change the disposition of the heavens, those who run across the seas, the poet Horace said. But there are seas, and there are means to go across them, as there are also anchors to stabilize the ship.

The journey could be a subterfuge to slow down change. It could also be the opportunity you need. If your house is in good order, undertake it. Sail forth!

FIVE OF GOLDS

•

A blaring light bursts in, intruding on you who had thirsted for it. The thousand complications of life step aside and open the way to the luminosity of the oracle.

There is no other truth than the moment's. You know what it is, you can see it. Set no obstacles to it: today, now, accept this truth. See how magnificent it is, how natural, how *obvious*.

Set your house in order. Calm yourself down. Open your window. You will immediately recognize the truth because, just as light does, truth changes everything without transforming anything. The furniture around you is still the same furniture, the walls the same walls. But everything you see is different from what it was in the dark, in the half light of that arduous hour before dawn.

Listen.

Do not crumple your soul into its illusions. Seek freedom from the shadows of your confusion. You will recognize yourself as you exist in the Universe, by your own right, just as the stars in the sparkled night, just as the snowfall which, weightless, crushes everything.

•

Careful! Careful with your aspirations!

You are blinded by a magnificent and tempting splendor. You are attracted to an ideal you know will be terrible; it calls you like a siren song. Your head says no; it tells you to resist that enticing call. But your heart tells you to go, to change your route, to run and fall for it.

Disconcerted, you now look all around you. The wealth of others makes you feel small and desolate, as if you had nothing to give. You look at the lights in the royal palace, lust for that glittery and well-heated palace emerging in the night of festivity and think yourself the most unhappy being on earth.

Now is the time to listen to the voice of your faith. The richness behind the golden windows exists in your soul just as your cold does. Beware of illusions.

SIX OF GOLDS

•

Do you remember how difficult decisions were? You had drawn lists: pros on one side, cons on the other. You had lain awake for nights debating with yourself what to do. You could reach no decision. You saw your future as a tiring climb, as a path filled with hazards, and all the while you pondered whether it led where you wanted to go.

Now, however, you know what you must do. You no longer need to fret about your actions. Complications, though they may be rich and positive, move aside. Hope beckons your journey. Hope gestures you to undertake it.

Of course, you will eventually come to a crossroads. And the crossroads will invite you to sit and think, and to change, offering you forgetfulness.

Then, after the crossing you will find another. You must again sit down. Address a prayer to the gods; they are the only beings to whom forgetting is allowed.

Change makes a labyrinth of life. In the center of the labyrinth—should we ever reach it—there is a monster ready to devour our innocence.

There are times when we can let go of the boat's rudder, but we can never forget.

•

Aw, come on. Let go. Open your hand, release your tight fist, and drop the coins. See how eagerly they are received, how they are grabbed away in a flash to be lustily revered by their new owners. As the captors scurry away, you may glimpse the greedy glitter in the rushing eyes. "Is this all?" they'll ask, sneering at your generous gift. That may be all you'll ever see of their gratitude, but is that glimmer of satisfaction not a thousand times brighter than the gold you gave them?

The money in your bank accrues on your fear: your fear of disease, as if health could be bought; your fear of poverty, as if all others were to be as ungenerous as you have been; your fear of loneliness, as if that lusterless gold were your only attraction; your fear of death, as if death never came to the opulent. The coins in your purse weigh you down.

Your giving makes you rich, only your giving.

SEVEN OF GOLDS

•

The branches of a tree rooted in my past darken the world upon me and blind me to my merit. I must pause now, and accept this gloom. The air around me thickens with the bad breath of failure, and I can think only of the effort expended on building this arbor—my heavily crafted failure, my strong-willed woe. Or is it all mine? Didn't I have partners in this construction? Why did I let the Bull of my mediocrity lead the way? What made me surrender to the Saturn of my reluctance?

I must search the eyes of those beasts, scan the skies for the stars of Taurus and the glow of the planets, and accept the strength of those I have nurtured inside me. Only thus may the radiance of my offering lighten my way.

I must take a moment to observe the fruits of my work. I have explored many pathways and, with each exploration, gained in experience. My road is not ended, nor its dangers and adventures. I will again swing in the perplexity of the unknown. But this is the hour for remorseless recollection.

I must pause in particular on those moments that seemed wasted. All those appeasing words I gave someone who wouldn't listen, all those projects that never came to anything, all those lessons that were never applied, all that patience.

•

Ah, how many acquisitions, how many goods, how much wealth! What paralyzing satisfaction! We count our coins: Gold!

We cool the tips of our fingers caressing the magic surface of our coins. Ah! Seven ounces of gold! We make lists. We turn our backs to the sky and count the coins yet to come. How many more? We *want*. Our craving puts weight on our breath. We grovel, yearning for more.

Shall we fill our lives with gold?

But, oh, let us not smother the voice reminding us half our journey is over. There is no infinite. Let us not be fooled by ambition.

EIGHT OF GOLDS

•

Isn't it a delight when we begin to see the fruits of our effort?

The time has come to give thanks, to look at the objects around us and acknowledge their existence, the company that keeps us, the service they give us. And there are so many things! At this very moment I give thanks for the bottle of ink, the smooth table on which I write, the lamp that lets me see, these old photographs that keep me company. In every thing I hear the effort of others, of everyone in history: their inventions, their exertions, their glories, their sorrows, even the pining echoes of their failures. And all the work I have done in my life is added to the waves of existence on earth and to the ocean of shared remembrance.

It is time to push my work ahead, to plunge into the efforts of the community, into the universe.

•

But tedium comes, nevertheless. Your own goods seem dull to you. Everything around you is far too organized—no leaks in your basement, no children to fuss about, no colleagues to test your patience, no blizzards to make you bundle up—and you are held back by lethargy, unwilling to make any changes. You feel as loath to push on as to pull back. Your only opportunity, you think, lies in feeding your routine. As usual. As usual.

You are condemned to your order and to your wealth; a Midas without glow, weighed down by the chains of rote, enslaved by prosperity. Such is your game now.

You must traverse this bog of stillness. In the meanwhile, rejoice in the gold of your chains.

NINE OF GOLDS

•

This is the moment of culmination, the moment of success. Your triumph.

But—you will say—but I haven't finished my work! I still need to put the final touches to it, rectify some important detail, apply the varnish...

Yes, we know. Your work is not completed, but it is almost there. This is your moment, your secret victory. Now you know you can do it! Later, when you have finished, you'll enjoy the satisfaction and will go out to celebrate. Then perhaps the laurel garland will hide the emptiness of accomplishment. Now you are quenched by your work, there is no separation between you and your work, you are all given to it like a lover.

Your triumph is now, not later, not at the end.

And nevertheless, you have to complete your work.

•

... to fall asleep inside a peaceful shelter, stretched out on soft rugs in between satin-lined pillows! To caress silk and damask, and see the wavering lamplight projecting playful shadows on the lattice. To observe the column of smoke rising from the tip of the incense stick and smell its fragrance as your thoughts soften and turn and become an embracing dream.

Everything around you exudes a sedate cooing, a sensual confusion, a protective disorder, a dimming parenthesis.

You may be like the falcon who, its head hidden by the hood, waits clawed to the hunter's leather glove. There is some tautness to the moment; you will be stripped of its blandness as of an illusion. For as soon as the hunter removes the hood you will dash after your prey, your beak anticipating the taste of blood.

PAGE OF GOLDS

•

Today's a holiday. The work is done. The Page of Golds is going out on a long walk. The world is hers. All roads are open and the clouds have dispersed. Today's not a day for responsibilities. On her way, the Page comes to a junction: she may undertake any of the seven roads offered her. Which one does she fancy? It doesn't matter, really. What matters is that she's out on her walk, that her legs are ready. The breeze on her face, the air in her lungs, and the faith in her heart all invite her to the walk.

She does not know how long her journey will be; ten days or ten years—or ten minutes. But it doesn't matter. The golden beach, or the forest of pines, or—why not—the seven-story mountain. Alone, with a dollar in her pocket—all she needs—the Page of Golds jaunts along the road of her passion.

•

Alone, and shiny. Your shoes are polished; a polite smile dawdles on your lips.

Careful! Who can you give your treasure to? What can you buy with your coin, with your smile?

You could purchase the routine of a burdensome bed, but you know you can't buy love. It could happen that, instead of buying a house, you acquire a prison. Or that, rather than emerging to the freedom of the fields, you embark on an adverse voyage, too fast-paced for you, leading where you do not need to go.

Beware of the driver of the machine. Do not undertake any journey that is not your own.

KNIGHT OF GOLDS

•

Feel the life on your horse's neck as you caress it. With all your offensive and defensive weapons, you know you could not go on without your horse, with just your strength.

And now you know you have to go on, yes, now, now that you have all your weapons and have come out into the fields having declared your mission.

But even though you have a road to follow—the road you yourself have chosen—you feel puzzled and open to the world. You know that your mission will no longer tell you whether to turn right or left. And you don't know who might come to your encounter: you might dismount and kneel before a solitary flower between patches of receding snow, or raise your visor when you see a shepherd and, with your helmet, offer him a drink of fresh water from the stream—or you will spur your horse against another knight.

Your path is full of turns and adventures. Yet it is as if you had made your path, and brought about all its jolts and wonder, and invited all the intrusions and discoveries—your path eternal in its every moment. Your passing, your alongness and aloneness, taking you where you are to go, enriched with the hope of reaching the castle that is your home.

•

The setting sun you pursue determinately is always further beyond. No matter how resolutely you ride towards the west, night will always get you first.

Has your mount perchance deceived you? Have all your preparations been in vain? Has a mischievous god concealed the North Star? Is it the hooves of another horse you hear, or the heaving of your own heart?

What do you feel when you press your calves against the beast, when your fingers choke the leather of the reins, when your spurs make your animal's belly bleed while your chin presses forth against the iron of its tophelm cage?

Many times we clench our teeth and tense our eyes. We have wished so hard for things without knowing that we did not want them!

KING OF GOLDS

•

How resplendent everything around you is! The sunset sky sputters golden dust. You perceive in yourself, now, the fruits of your efforts, the process of your life, the untiring march of history. And also your permanence, your fidelity to that core of being unperturbed by all your experiences and changes. The world shows itself to you rich and full.

Others will seek your advice and request your guidance. And you'll give it to them, because you no longer mind; the truer the advice the more you love them. Calculation is behind you. You know you have more than enough with what's yours and need search no further. You shall give, knowing that giving is not conceding; and your giving, asking for nothing in return, will make you richer.

Now that you no longer need it to be present, the wealth of the world will be in you. The world is full; you may not sit down. Yes, you now sit atop the Wheel of Fortune. From your vantage point you see how all other positions on the wheel are defined by this top one. From the summit, you know it doesn't matter if you fall, because you are not enslaved by the effort that brought you here. You are at the very top. You reign. You reign now, out of love, and you know nothing else matters.

•

Oh, how heavy the crown and how cumbersome the robes! These shoes are too delicate and will prevent me from getting too far from the throne. I no longer laugh at the buffoon that kept me amused.

My life is altogether too dazzling, too golden, too warm. The roadways are all too familiar; my wealth is too solitary.

What would happen if I undressed and went out into unknown country? If I started to howl like a dog to the full moon? If I gave up the glory of my burden to follow the anointed guide of my own happiness?

The oxen of my will won't advance me. Nor can I feel the silk of my festival robe over my armor. Even my scepter weighs like a mace. Who really is this person choked by wealth and symbols?

QUEEN OF GOLDS

•

The Queen sat on her throne and beckoned me to approach her. Even though she still cloaked herself with a mantle, her clothes seemed lighter, and indeed signs of spring appeared all around her. I came to her with a mixture of fear and devotion, but ready to give her all I had: my story. In response, she offered me a look into her golden mirror. I sought my reflection in it, and saw myself as if disfigured, different from what I had thought I looked like. There I saw a harsh figure, shiny eyes that looked at me with alien recognition, the burnt stare of the otherness of my self. I saw my seven sins not any less clear than my virtues. I looked at the image for a while. The picture in the mirror seemed distorted and I felt tempted at first to attribute its ugliness to the many bashes on the metal. But yet that pitiless portrait that stressed like a malicious caricature my worst traits, was a portrait of me. And more faithful than the smoothed-out illusion I had on my mind. I felt horror, and then rebellion. No; surely that is not me. It cannot be. Then I looked into the eyes of the Queen and saw no lies. Yes, that reflection was inescapably me, the new me I had been all along.

The Queen returned her mirror to her lap. Not very long ago that mirror was just a piece of metal, all bashed up, lying discarded on the side of the road.

•

Do not be afraid of the Queen of Golds. The expression you guess in her features is not sadness and certainly not disapproval. She gives; her gift might be the best you'll have received. But you are the one to set the value of her gift.

Do you find your acceptance of her gift costly? Do you perhaps think that the gift is worthless if given to you? Do you still need others to set the true price to her present, even though it is not for them?

The sadness of expression you see in the Queen's face is your own. You have come to yourself but do not yet know it. And you don't know it because it is only now that you are ready, primed to know it.

What is all this? What does the Queen's oracle mean?

You may be tired of these questions, and rightly so, for your exploration has been long. Quit now and be happy for what you have achieved. But if something pushes you to further knowledge, turn your ear inwards and listen to the voices. In any case, give your soul the bread of wisdom: silence.

THE GREATER SECRETS

0
THE FOOL

•

No dishes to wash, no fences to paint, no bills to pay or schedules to keep, no self to tie the moments together but simply a burst of being in everything—this is the time of our innocence before the fall into adulthood. Why talk about that time in the past? The present belongs to no past and to no future, only to the selfless Fool, a child of one's own fantasy, the ungreedy eyes of wonderment. Or to the repeated timelessness of never-never.

So the Fool walks on with a rose in his left hand and the stick with the bundle of all he has in his right. All around him, time holds his life for ransom, but the Fool has no feeling for time's conscriptions. His moments are his, to be drunk with a child's careless attention. Drunk with the timelessness of the now but egged on by the dog of his conformity, the Fool finds himself at the edge of a precipice. The sun is shining on his back. Between the cragginess of the road that issues from the ferny hill and the certainty of his fall, this moment sparkles with lightness.

And so we have fallen and forgotten that life is a slippery series of oblivions. We've striven to grab and shackle life, our gaze avidly projected outwards, running after the objects of our desire. We've held on to the anxiety of work with expectations of reward and perhaps glory. And so we've sought to leave everything tidied up, pasted in the scrapbook of our memory. We've asked the sun, the clouds, the sky, and even the rose in its wilting, to step back and remain there, orderly like the books on the shelves of a library, glorious like a butterfly pinned just above its Latin name, beheaded like the statue of Nike.

That has been our adult folly, our ego-full wish for the present to be the past, and for now to be eternity. In our struggle we were to be sovereign among the many, not merely good but better, forever out of breath in an aimless quest for permanence.

There is one thing ahead of the Fool: the precipice of an assured fall. For indeed, the Child will crash into the gully of a sane existence, and, no longer golden in the eyes of time, do his penance of ambition and remorse. Yes, the Fool will fall into time and nothingness and remain there.

Unless...

I
THE MAGICIAN

•

Weave yourself into my words, you Fool.

I am the words, or what you make with these words. You can imagine me. You can make me woman or man, but make me fearless; make me rich or poor, but make me loving; black or white, but make me open; real or dreamed, but alive. Make me like you and you will have made yourself like me: a mirror in which you see yourself as a stranger.

The infinite is my crown: I am the Magician. Behold on the table before me a gold coin, a club of wood, a cup and a sword. A belt in the form of a snake girds my white tunic. I am the juggler dressed in a coat of red and ready for the journey. With raised hand, defying all fear, I burn both ends of the candle.

I—a word now meaning also you—am about to embark on my journey inward. The road winds towards my center. I shall trust no guide, but only the road itself as I follow it. I will trust no guide, for to trust a guide would be to give up the journey and make it merely an excuse for an arrival. And our journey ends nowhere; it is a journey nowhere.

The journey must be as long as the road, which knows no end. The road, which I cannot name, will change me. And I know that my inevitable transformation will alter the road. Now everything is possible. My present repose is but a step in the dance of life. Hermes and Mercury are my gods, the two faces of my god. It is they who take the dead to Hades, they who are the keepers of my secret. I am, and I can, because I have received their breath.

Step into the world with me, let us search for the resonances of words we have already heard inside. When we see a flower, we shall think "flower"; when we see a cloud, we shall think "cloud". In the same manner, during the journey we are undertaking, as we say words such as "Priestess", "Empress", "Emperor", and "Hierophant", we shall encounter these characters and make them ours, as they make us theirs.

The road opens before us. Strength and lightness are our best gifts. Strength, lightness of foot... and a few drops of deceit, the cipher of the juggler's art. For I am a juggler; my destiny is play and theatre, in a word, deceit. I am the flesh of my mask and of your mask, its scaffolding of spirit, the confluence of invisible truths and impalpable lies. Flesh and spirit come together in me; of their coupling are born joke and yoke, function and junction, the wheel and the road.

II
THE HIGH PRIESTESS

•

Careful: beware of knowing too soon.
Beware of divination.

From its wintry abode in Cancer, the moon announces growth and discloses fecundity. The almond trees have bloomed, but not yet the pomegranates. They will open later, at the death of summer whose birth I now feel.

I am Esther, daughter of Ishtar, mother of Iseult. My gift to you will be your patience: the art of waiting and fretting, the art of pain and of passion. May the moon that brightens our nights save you from the burden of foreknowledge.

Be careful. You must learn, and before you learn you must study, and before you study you must read. The law is written on these parchments; you must know their language before you study them, know them before you know me.

Can you find your way on this floor of alternating tiles? What thread will guide you? You eye the veil held by the two columns behind me. But you must be prudent. You don't know what potion my goblet holds, or against whom I'll brandish my

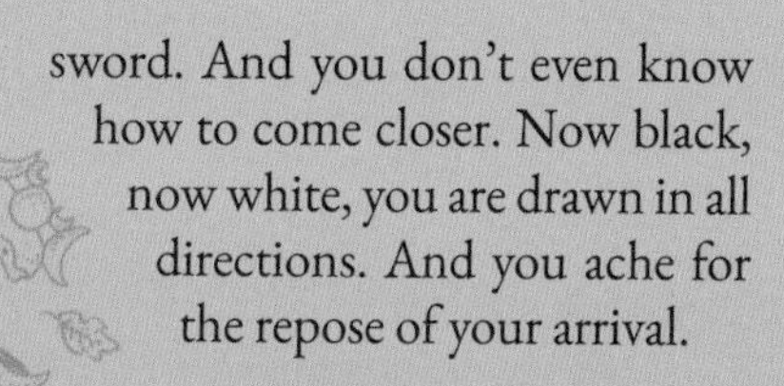

sword. And you don't even know how to come closer. Now black, now white, you are drawn in all directions. And you ache for the repose of your arrival.

Let my veil be. Look at it and accept it as your own shroud of ignorance. You cannot rend that which you do not own. You cannot overcome the obstacle without the steely piercings of your pains and the humility that will make you accept my libation.

Kneel and pray. Make me yours as your own prudence.

III
THE EMPRESS

•

Juggler, stop here. What else could the longing of your heart desire? Little else, I can tell you now: some spiritual foolery, empty dreams thundering with vanity, the mangy dogs of your ambition.

I offer you, instead, a world rich with gifts. I offer you the empire of the senses, my empire. Look, juggler, at the light of this summer morning; the rising sun reveals a golden dust and the nightingale spins its fruity song. Among the trees, the stream discloses its fish. My wheat ripens round us: this winter, by the fire, we will enjoy the placidity my well-stocked granaries give.

Touch the soft satin of my bedding. My hands are artful. You can own the excitement their touch will give.

I shall take off this crown of diamonds and this scepter. Remove my tunic, see me naked, embrace me, quench yourself in me. Melt into this thirsty body. Let yourself go. Free yourself in your fructification. When you have given your self to the love of the body—the whole world suspended against the plunge of famished time—your own spittle will be the manna of glory. You will be sated: with your power, with your life, and with all that you can find, sense, only in me, in us.

Love. Convert your life to this moment of joy.

IV
THE EMPEROR

•

Majesty is silence, majesty is solitude. Sublimity, once attained, is as unbreathable as the air on the highest peaks. When you aspire to my throne, you aspire to the seat of a supreme and choking will. Wretched are they who sit there forever. Yet you must aspire to a throne like mine, the Ithaca of your longings and of your delays. You must come to me to find the meaning of your wanderings.

The paths of the ascent are many; a multitude of symbols mark their way. Be warned: the apprenticeship is hard, only your dream of glory will help you keep your step. Each time you stumble, you will have to repeat to yourself that it is not the mountain you seek that fatigues you, far away and imposing, rosy with sunset snow; it is a grain of sand in your shoe, a grain of doubt in your mind. Pity those who give up the mountain because of a grain of sand. Pity those whose sorry science converts their lives into a purgatory of daily comforts and certainties.

Some, blinded by the western sun, think the stone in my necklace an emerald, green and luminous: the stone of Hermes, the Magician's god, your god, the god of secrets and of theft. In their rush, these strive to the glittering riches of my palace. They will spare no sacrifice to attain my glacial possessions and dream themselves satiated and wise.

Do not be fooled. My treasure dies with me.

What hangs from my necklace is a pearl. In the center of the pearl lies a grain of sand, not unlike those that so many times have slipped into your sandal while you were on the way. As the pearl is made of tears and secretion around the grain of sand, so will your knowledge be the fruit of your suffering. For it is the road to the summit, and not the high erected throne, that will give you your only wisdom, born of the saliva of aspiration, weaned on tears, taught by delays, trained by the many distractions along the way. Yet this knowledge is impossible without my silent and solitary sovereignty.

V
THE HIEROPHANT

•

Call me Archpriest, or High Priest, or, better yet, Pope. Help me sit here in between my two columns. Hand me my triple cross. See? It has seven endings.
You have arrived, my child. It all adds up now.

I am the fourth character you've met. If you add—go on, why don't you?—this four to the three of the triangle, you'll have the seven endings of my cross. You can't get more conclusive than seven. But let's take another count. I am the fourth character you've met so far. Of course with you I make a fifth... Aw, come on, don't stare at me. Have you forgotten how to count? Do you no longer remember what the numbers mean? Five is for the magic pentacle, the five-pronged star of humanity. Don't you know the meaning of my name? I have to be patient with you, that's obvious. "He who shows the sacred." All symbols converge in me, the star of your perplexity.
You have arrived.

I see what you're thinking. You find me strange, almost repulsive, don't you? I'm fat and I'm sweaty. You think my message corrupt. You see in my figure the sublimation of your trickeries. What do you say? Am I saint or charlatan? Or can't you see through your mask? Did I hear you mutter something?

Some of my counselors tell me that perfection is an aberration. They may be right.

I'll make a deal with you. (What, you didn't expect this kind of talk from me?) Okay, I'll give you the Mysteries of one week: the sloth symbolized by the moon of Monday; the wrath of Mars and the envy of Mercury for Tuesday and Wednesday. What? Speak louder, child. You say that's Tiu and Woden? By Jove, you may be right! But let's leave Jove and his greed for Thursday, and Thor be damned! Oh,

I see, you're going to contest me Venus's lust for Friday in the name of that old hag Frigg who never heard we'd moved to Rome. Do as you please. Although perhaps we'll agree on the avarice of Saturn for Saturday and on the pride of the Sun on the day of the Lord. Yeah, take a week.

You think I'm being obscure? As I said, kid, take a week. Sleep on it, seven times. Or triple the experience to follow in the footsteps of the Thrice-Greatest.

VI
THE LOVERS, A DIALOGUE

•

There is always some hell in Paradise.

Yes, the wings of the archangel Michael are made of fire, the apples on the tree of the knowledge of good and evil are made of fire. The serpent crawling up its trunk is our bond: every choice creates a destiny. The zenith is nothing more than the illusory balance between dawn and dusk.

The more perfect, the more delicate, and the more subtle the balance, the more unstable it becomes. Our life as lovers unfolds in the little death of sex. Now, before us, we have all the possibilities of life. We are now both what we were yesterday and what we shall be tomorrow. Our union buds out into transformation, transformation blooms out into change.

To love is a delicate thing. Only when I love do I open the rose of my loneliness. I have come to feel so alone, so all-one, that now I can surrender to joy: to the joy of the other, who with me knows nothing of me; to the joy of myself, who in union knows nothing of the other. We are a plural of one lover. There is no love without its seed of aloneness. Nothing without the seed of its opposite.

Paradise is always a paradise lost. The fallen angel—the most beautiful of all angels—was the one who, in the fall, invented paradise. And on the tree of life there are twelve flowers: flowers of marriage and of divorce, forgiveness and reconciliation, flowers of love.

VII
THE CHARIOT

•

Not a bad machine this, really, although it might not impress the technologically conscious young. But then, who knows what impresses the young? You must come for a ride in it; the suspension is excellent. And you won't believe the upholstery: it's plush and satiny, and may I fit as comfortably in my coffin. I can't give you a ride now, though; these inscrutable beasts that pull my chariot aren't going to move. I suppose they have earned their rest. Look at them: one is black, one white; one wants to go left, the other right. They don't see eye to eye.
I can't remember what made me choose them.

I've had an errant destiny, that's for sure. Home, to me, has always been where I'm not. There, there, there... I never felt any place was my place, any house my house. And yet I pine for a home. That pining puts my true home always yonder. There, just over there. One more tunnel, one more bend in the road. My journey keeps pushing my house away, beyond, always beyond. It may not be far now... just at the horizon, I think. That's where the sun is going, anyhow, but my beasts demand their midday siesta. They are always delaying me. Will I ever get home?

VIII
FORTITUDE

•

I'll tell you how difficult it all could be. Go research and draw out a plan. Clench your fists and make up your mind. Be determined. Be prepared. Mistrust your enemy; be sure to assume only malice from him. Remember every defeat from the past. Flush your brain with the bile of resentment, cloud your vision with the blood of vengeance. All the studies you have undertaken and all the plans you have devised are making you fear a new situation, even a total reversal. You have spent much time and effort, I know, calculating your every step, foreseeing every move. But you are still afraid an earthquake will crumble the road before you or even under your feet. You are baffled. You tremble. You are scared of your own armor—and you will destroy the world, and yourself, before admitting that you are afraid.

I'll tell how easy it all could be. Trust your strength. Your hand and your arms will find their path. Let serenity, delicacy, and softness guide them. See how scared is your enemy under his boasting. He will win if he is to win, no matter how taken you are with your own reasons.

First thing: you must dress. Bathe, and then examine your clothes laid out on the bed. Once dressed, don't forget the ornaments.

Samurai always prepare for battle by dressing up. Impeccably, as do bullfighters. They dress slowly, concentrating on every moment, as in prayer.

Then think that your victory matters only now, for afterwards all will return to its course. Feel your feet planted on the ground and stand for your self and for your center, not for a square of earth that never did belong to you.

IX
THE HERMIT

•

Some call me taciturn, fussy. Always alone, they say. They look on me with suspicion and curse me for this love that spurts out to no one. For them, I am a polluter and a curmudgeon, forever searching for what cannot be had. Indeed I have scrounged through the stacks of libraries hoping to find the book not yet read by anyone. But they say I see nothing but the page, the blanks between the letters. I keep records, but no one reads my small hand. The library always closes before I have finished and then, grabbing my staff, I leave for the empty night. I walk dragging my feet on the floor slabs. My head hangs down. I appear older than I am. And I cover myself, I hide.

According to others, I am the guide who,
lamp in hand, shows the way from the
top of the mountain: I am Virgil,
helping the poet descend into
darkness in order to help him to
rise; Tiresias, who knows the
secrets of men and women;
Aesculapius who, with his
staff, will tame the serpent
of rebel knowledge.

I am both master and
beggar. The cape that keeps
me warm mutters to my
ear. No one sees me, but all
look at me. No one pays me
attention, but many follow
me. I am hermit and enigma,
the light of the wasteland in
the cold of the night. A star
sputters. All the rest is dark.

I have grown so old in my studies that
I came to forget what I was looking for.
Thus has the light receded from my skin
to my old eyes, still searching and still hoping

to find my love and my suffering, my passion and my patience. Now I can tell you, for I see in you at once the sage and the fool I have been and am: what I didn't know I was looking for was my passion. While I didn't know what kind of fire burned inside me, I was unable to offer love, even receive love from anyone. I searched and searched, seeking without what was within; yet I knew that once I found what I love in me—my passion and my calling—I will be able to cast aside my hermit's mantle, for my own light will warm me aplenty. This is my story, this is how I have eddied into seclusion bidding hasty retreats and bitter goodbyes, angry at the shadows that chased me.

X
THE WHEEL OF FORTUNE
(from the Magician's diary)

•

How obtuse, how obnoxious, the squealing of that Wheel. Doesn't anybody ever oil it?

I didn't mind the figures around it, with their captain Janus, the two-faced god who opens and closes time. I didn't mind the blind destiny that exalts and abases, nor the passage of time which makes all sovereignty and all hope for glory ephemeral. Or the sudden reversal, or the unexpected and undeserved elevation. No. The hateful dullness of the Wheel lies in its thorough aping, in its perfect reflection of the stuff I am made of—of what I am and of what you are, a mirror that disrobes us of all illusions.

T
A
R
O

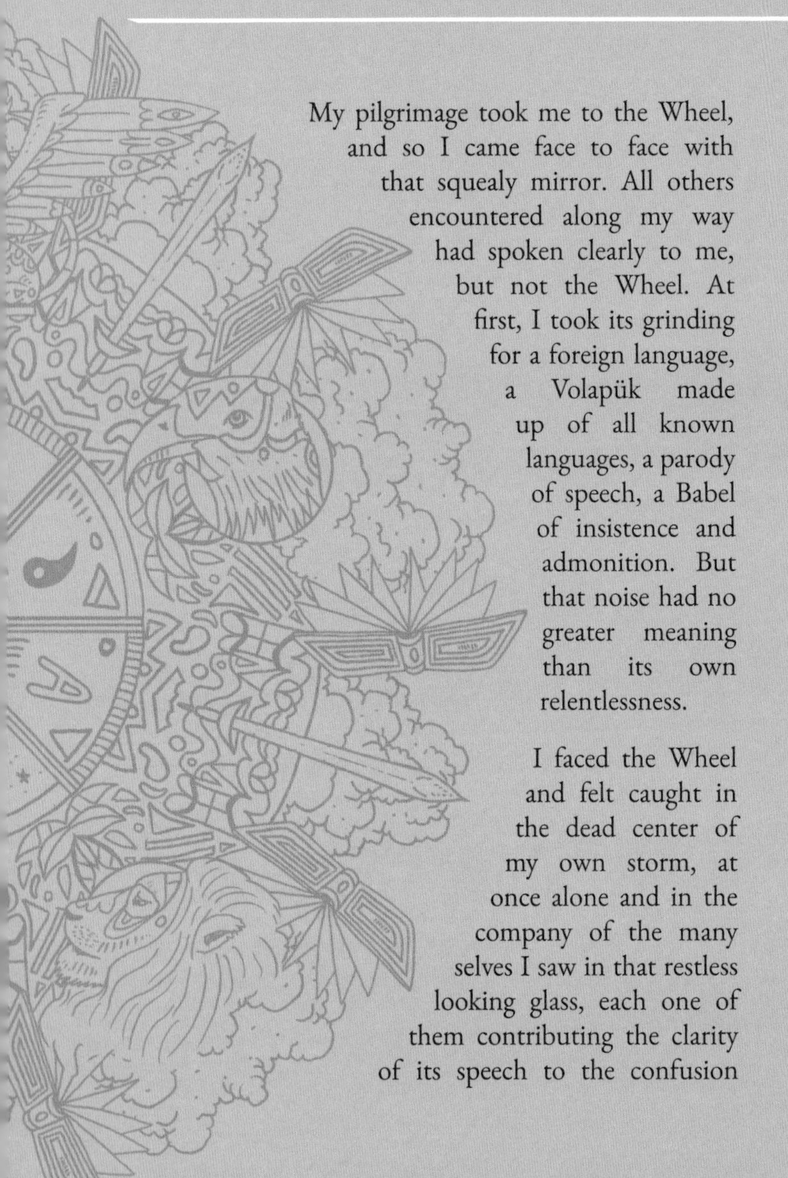

My pilgrimage took me to the Wheel, and so I came face to face with that squealy mirror. All others encountered along my way had spoken clearly to me, but not the Wheel. At first, I took its grinding for a foreign language, a Volapük made up of all known languages, a parody of speech, a Babel of insistence and admonition. But that noise had no greater meaning than its own relentlessness.

I faced the Wheel and felt caught in the dead center of my own storm, at once alone and in the company of the many selves I saw in that restless looking glass, each one of them contributing the clarity of its speech to the confusion of the squeals. At one point I felt I could decipher some sounds: "You are and at once you have been and will be: nothing makes sense without the others." I thought I understood: I am many and I insist in vain on being one; I am because I have been and, at the same time, I am not without that which is not: present, past, and future make one another, unceasingly.

In the middle of the road the Wheel continued its grinding. Nothing is without being everything, I thought: no poor without rich, no joy without pain, no triumph without failure, no god without devil. No life without death.

These are the untiring, the tiresome squeals of the hub of the Wheel, the vertigo of its upheavals, the headiness and despair of its circumvolutions. The taxing predictability of its ill-greased cycles rubbing relentlessly on the hard axis of life.

Meanwhile, at the cardinal points, the four bearers of signs stood ready to spread the news—the old news forever trying to make sense of time. Having come this far, with no road that is not traced by a wheel, with no wheel possible without a road, I had to go on. And I knew that somehow, for all the confusion of the scene and in spite of all its repetitiveness, I had been changed.

XI
JUSTICE

•

Don't greet me when you're wounded. Don't fawn on me behind the plumage of your hurt. Don't mince about with childish smiles. Don't fatigue me with your excuses. And don't rush me. The sun has not bleached the parchments I told you to read and the rain has not bled them. They are as clear now as they have ever been, but the tears in your eyes hide them from you. Enough procrastinations, enough stumbling.

Rise. Throw away that cap, the timid shield of your shame. Stand and look at me, arms at your sides and both feet planted on the ground. Look at me.

Don't you recognize me now?

You are not going to see what's behind the veil between my two columns if first you don't put all your actions on my scales for weighing. Every one of them, however long it takes. I want what you have given and what you have taken, what you have wished for and what you have enjoyed, what you have eaten and what you have left, what you have bought and what you have sold, what you have broken and repaired, what you have cleaned and defiled; your gifts and your thefts, your rest and your effort, your laughter and your groans, your days and your nights, your lies and your avowals, your hopes and your fears, your poetry and your curses, your poison and your blood.

See—it balances out. Now, in full acknowledgement, come close and look at yourself in the steel of my sword to see if the veil can be rent.

XII
THE HANGED MAN

•

No, I am not Narcissus, even though I look like one who dipped his head in dead Cairo's henna. I *am* upside-down.

Most passers-by avert their gazes; you are one of the few who has dared look at me. People see me as an aberration, a lost soul, even a traitor. They laugh at me. "Don't listen to him," they'll tell you, "he's a fool. He thinks he's invented the wheel. Ha!"

And others lament: "How tragic! He will pluck out his eyes, for grief has already seized his heart. Pity him who glows with the light of his errors. He's condemned to his lights as if he were a firefly. There's nothing he can do but get what he deserves."

Yet I see what
they don't, what
you don't, what
your uprightness
and apparent freedom
prevent you from seeing.
And what their dime-
store dogmatism has gotten
them. Upright blindfolk, the whole
lot! What team are they members of?
Does their banner read Faith or Freedom?

Freedom, you say? And so what? You shun the comfort of obedience for the pride of your anguish. Big deal! Do you really expect your reasons to give flesh to your visions? You value your findings only if they accord with your expectations; that is your punishment. Nothing will surprise you.

You will not see
these fruits here
as flowers striving
for their return to
the deep. You will know
nothing of the parents of
the ocean, of the ascending
light of the sun's rays, of the
darkness of the infinite, of the bent fate
of all returnings.

Rules and logic will always bind your passage. Unless you hang and dangle, unless you challenge the wrath of all, and suffer their self-righteous betrayal, you'll never transcend the ordinary. Dare look under the skirts of Maya. Cross your legs, hide your tricks. Blend your prudence with some impudence. Dive!

XIII
DEATH
(from the diary)

•

I have never seen anyone looking more tired than Death. She advances slowly on a horse that drags its feet. As she passes, all falls. Only the wind lends a quiver to the few dry leaves remaining on the trees. The sky is gray and frost the only flower.

All things lose their being. The crow caws no more, the leopard curses its spots, the dove crawls on the ground, the air no longer wants to be the air. You make no effort to be yourself. I make no effort to be me. Everything unties, everything hangs limp. Death advances, seemingly indifferent, her gaze lost in the distance. At its muffled passing all is submission, all stoops, all falls to the ground, will-less.

But all transformation needs Death's passage. When we realize the change we have suffered, when we feel transformed, when we are reborn to a new mortality, it is then that we see Death. At this darkest of places along my road, sleep overtook me. Sleep and a dream:

An ocean liner stands over the oily waters of the port. A throne studded with precious stones shines over a heap of garbage on the dock. The hero raises his blood-stained hands to the crown on his head, but he cannot remove it. His lover, insomniac in her cabin, lies belly-down on the bed. She presses her guilt into the pillow. The hero feels glued to his throne. An ermine mantle falls over his blue tunic. On his hands gloves of golden velvet, with embroidered crosses, and over one finger, an onyx ring. The waters of the port appear heavy. Without moving, the liner fills the air with a blow of its siren. The lights of the luxury cabins flicker on the waters. In the night I hear the pitter-pat of steps approaching.

XIV
TEMPERANCE

•

There is a spring in every season. Quiet angels like me appear anywhere, unannounced. We are here to ward off the evil that gathers like a storm all around you. Yet we have made no plans, we plot no schemes, we have no program, no purpose, we hope for nothing: we are.

Think of how essential solitude is, think of those long walks in the woods, those aimless walks that have brought you back your calm. Hasn't roaming by yourself fed you much better than the crazed joy of company? I am that kind of solitude, Temperance. I am your angel; trust me.

Put on comfortable clothes, and, when your cup is full, pour it into a more capacious one. Do not mistake Temperance for sacrifice.

The world might appear cruel, but you must know that, even if it does not seem evident, the universe follows a course implacably determined which is the course it requires, regardless of the rickety reasons of human will.

Your will leads to absurdity. Do not push the river, for it flows by itself: do not expect the cart to push the horse. The power at your fingertips can be inebriating. Try to use it to conquer the world and you will see that your fate has conquered you. You will be neither Magician nor Fool, just a cog in a senseless machine, unable to stop, unable to think.

The same goes for diet plans; what is real is your hunger and your thirst. Bite hard, when you have to eat, and do not be afraid of slurping when you need to drink. Look at your excesses, now that you have comfortable clothes on, and consider the reasons they obey. Let go, my child, let go. Release your hold of world and self, release the grasp that tightens you from your own abdomen, release and soar. This is what we angels of Temperance are all about.

XV
THE DEVIL

•

I have bad press and a German accent besides. So be it. The dogs bark whenever the king's coach goes by, as Goethe said. What I'd like to know is: Why am I singled out as pernicious when I am just a mirror along the road like all the others? You all come to me with your fears and that's what you see in me. Fear makes people dangerous, not me or my alleged bribes. Like dogs, you act your fiercest when you're afraid. People blame me, plaster me with signs—signs of your own fear—and declare me ugly, vituperous, obsessed, and foul-smelling. You people see your own ugliness in me as you do in others, then you are repulsed by it: there's nothing you hate more. You call your reflections your enemy and wage war against them. So be it, if that's what you want.

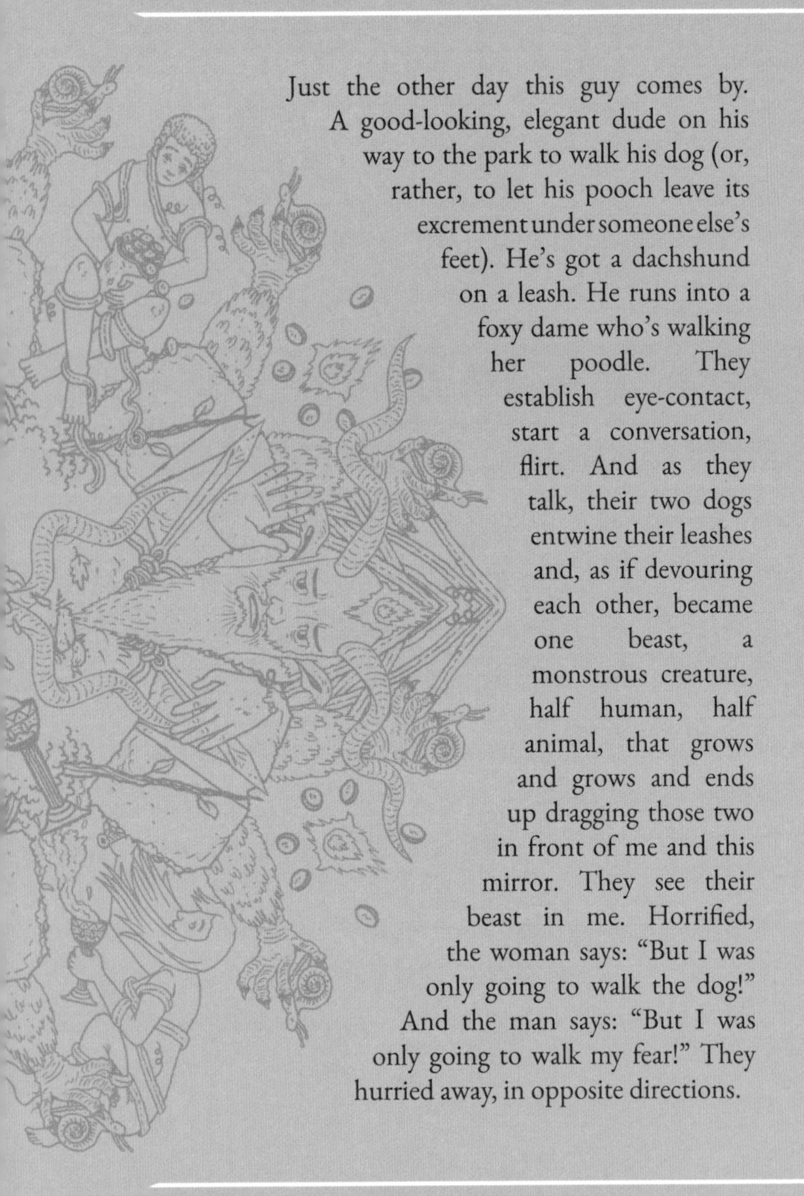

Just the other day this guy comes by. A good-looking, elegant dude on his way to the park to walk his dog (or, rather, to let his pooch leave its excrement under someone else's feet). He's got a dachshund on a leash. He runs into a foxy dame who's walking her poodle. They establish eye-contact, start a conversation, flirt. And as they talk, their two dogs entwine their leashes and, as if devouring each other, became one beast, a monstrous creature, half human, half animal, that grows and grows and ends up dragging those two in front of me and this mirror. They see their beast in me. Horrified, the woman says: "But I was only going to walk the dog!" And the man says: "But I was only going to walk my fear!" They hurried away, in opposite directions.

You too, you've seen me many times; whenever you were alone and wanted to run away from yourself but couldn't. You've seen me in your looking glass at home, confident that no one was observing you. You've walked to the full-length mirror in your room, and then become disgusted by what you saw, by the sagging and furrowing of your skin, or by your ungraceful muscle and bent skeleton, whatever. Your eyes, seeing me, have fixed on your ugliness, more horrible than anyone else's, the more disgusting the more yours.

You've rushed to put on your clothes, the most expensive in your wardrobe, done your face and your hair, looked again, in profile—no, the other side is better—tucked your stomach in, worked up to a smile, a grin.

And then you've begged for me to come and bribe you. No, not to make you beautiful; you never believed I could do that. Only to tell you that the body doesn't matter, that you have a soul, a beautiful soul, to talk to you about the mind and the spirit. To mutter in your ear over and over again that you have a soul and that it is the soul that matters, not the body.

The soul. The soul that demands effort, manipulation, negation and abnegation. Work. Yes, you've met me many times.

XVI
THE TOWER STRUCK BY LIGHTNING

•

Siste Viator: Stop a moment, traveler, and witness my crumbled pride. Lean on your cane and read the inscription in my stones. As you hurry away, be mindful that you must return to this place.

Siste Viator: It is a fine line that divides fear and joy. When you want to fix the happiness of living the moment and steady the letting go of the boat's oars, when you want to cement your joy and feel the assurance of its possession, when you want joy yours to keep, then joy eludes you. And it is solicitously replaced by uncertainty. And uncertainty becomes fear when you forget that all your steps in the world are nothing more than a wake frothy with uncertainty. The winds of doubt fill away the sails on the ship of life.

Siste Viator: Patches and arrangements often last longer than those things conscientiously built. Some things, held together by a little saliva, cling on. Buttons may hang for years from a single thread, a sentence read hurriedly at the newsstand may remain with you longer than a memorized text.

Siste Viator: Chance is the tatting in the web of fate. Jack hesitated before he made up his mind to go to the party, and once there almost decided not to talk to the woman. Yet he did, out of boredom. Jill might have been thinking of leaving the party early, but stayed. Jack and Jill might not have left together, but the party had made them feel lonely and sharing a taxi they felt adventurous. A billboard along the way prompted Jack to invite Jill over for a nightcap... Perhaps they wouldn't have ended up having sex. There might have been no fecundation. Perhaps that one chromosome would not have been Y. Perhaps the son... Life is all chance. All could be different. Or not be.

Siste Viator: Of one thing you can be sure: you will leave this world and your imprints will be erased.

Siste Viator: Here lie the tongues of the world, struck by the wrath of God.

XVII
THE STAR
(from the diary)

•

An unexpected light coming from a star surrounded by seven others—the numbers of the One and of the ALL—announced to me that I was entering the penultimate phase of my pilgrimage. The light of that star, light of revelation and discovery, fed on the darkness surrounding and defining it. Having met the five characters and passed the ten tests, I was to behold three manifestations of light: the Star, the Moon, and the Sun.

The Star had taken human form in the shape of a naked maiden pouring water from two jars. The maiden was Sophia—the feminine principal of all wisdom—or perhaps Venus, the rising-star goddess born in the waters.

I felt the cool of night under the springtime sky. Shredded clouds, the sky's bangs, recalled last winter's rains. I heard the nightingale's song. Of what color is this bird who sings at night? How far does it go in its migration? Where does it go? Everything was dry in the night around the birdsong introducing the pouring of the waters. Everything had been dry until the maiden came with her two jars of water. With one jar she fertilized the arid ground; with the other she renewed the waters in the pond.

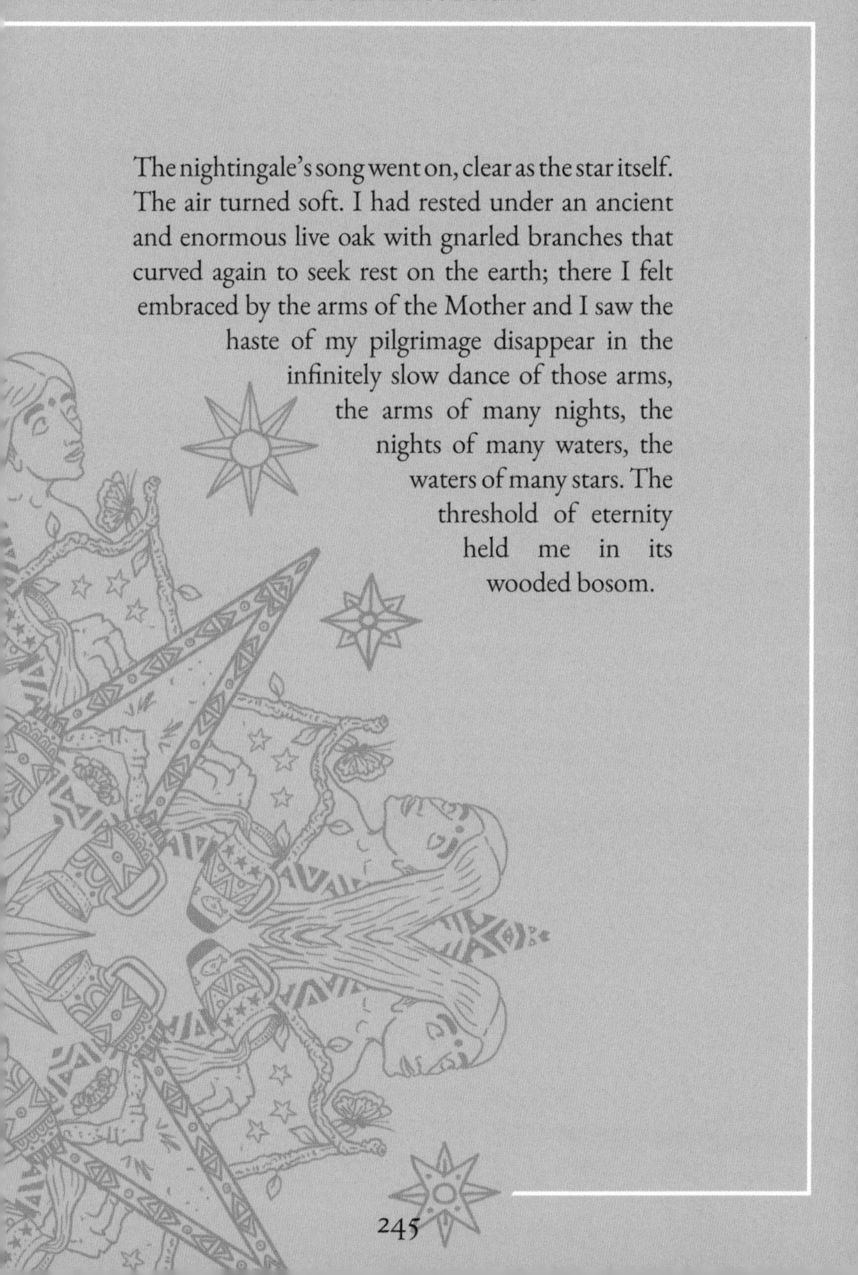

The nightingale's song went on, clear as the star itself. The air turned soft. I had rested under an ancient and enormous live oak with gnarled branches that curved again to seek rest on the earth; there I felt embraced by the arms of the Mother and I saw the haste of my pilgrimage disappear in the infinitely slow dance of those arms, the arms of many nights, the nights of many waters, the waters of many stars. The threshold of eternity held me in its wooded bosom.

XVIII
THE MOON

•

I am sure you have gone out in the fields under a full moon when things—the natural objects—appeared eternal. A carob or an olive tree outlines itself against the background of blue studded like a jeweler's prodigious masterwork. Everything has an air at once real and ghostly. From far away you hear the barking of a dog. The spurt of a motorcycle becomes present, increases to its zenith, then begins to die as it gets lost into mystery. Reality is the product of dream. You have the feeling that objects in nature—a rock, a bush, that very olive tree—are gulped by mystery as soon as your eyes move away. The dog's bark heard just now, is it not the howling of a wolf? The road before you vanishes in the hills outlined against a sky mottled with clouds.

My light
lends a baffling
glow to things
and transforms
everything, even the
taste of saliva in your
mouth. All that, during
the day, you think is yours,
I make strange, I make alien.

I, the luminous full Moon, whose light defeats the night's darkness, will remind you of the superficiality of your passage through this life. Your inevitable passing now becomes clear. You will pass and dwindle as the clouds do, your memory will be lost like the smoke from a chimney.

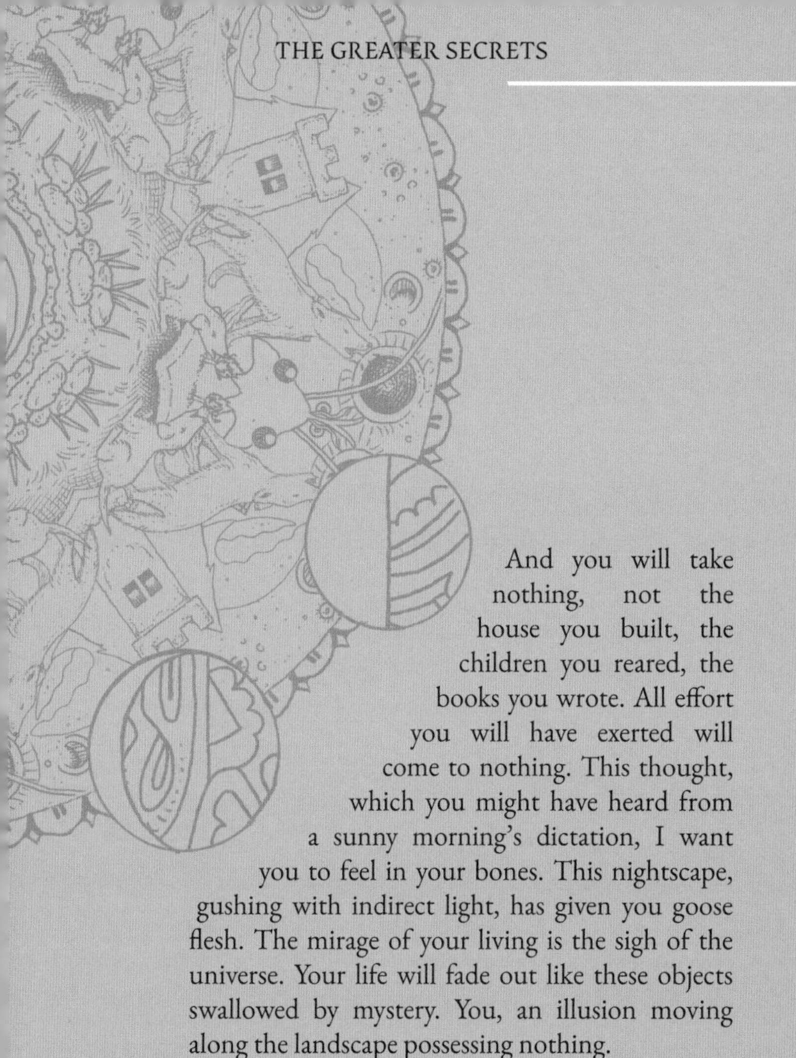

And you will take nothing, not the house you built, the children you reared, the books you wrote. All effort you will have exerted will come to nothing. This thought, which you might have heard from a sunny morning's dictation, I want you to feel in your bones. This nightscape, gushing with indirect light, has given you goose flesh. The mirage of your living is the sigh of the universe. Your life will fade out like these objects swallowed by mystery. You, an illusion moving along the landscape possessing nothing.

XIX
THE SUN

•

Take off your clothes! Take off your shoes! Come down to the beach at daybreak. The breeze makes the palms rustle. There is a glimmer on the perennial waves. The clarity is absolute. Even the shadow of your body radiates light.

The clarity is absolute.

The day is perfect. The thousand little things that go wrong make it complete. The sea is littered with dead seaweed. On the beach, shoeless, you've just stepped on a glob of tar; its insistent pulp clings to your toes. But you don't care. You accept the peskiness of the fly and the distraction of the mongrel sniffing your leg. Such is the world: always more beautiful than the perfect utopias contrived by your wishes.

A seagull that, with great effort, remained fixed in the air above you, dives in and emerges with a fish in its beak. The fish is too big and falls. The sun is up. You are.

Before you retake the road, pause again and pick up one of these daisies. Caress its white petals with your little finger; feel each petal surrender beneath your touch. Notice the unabatable weight of your indecision. Then begin pulling out the petals one by one.

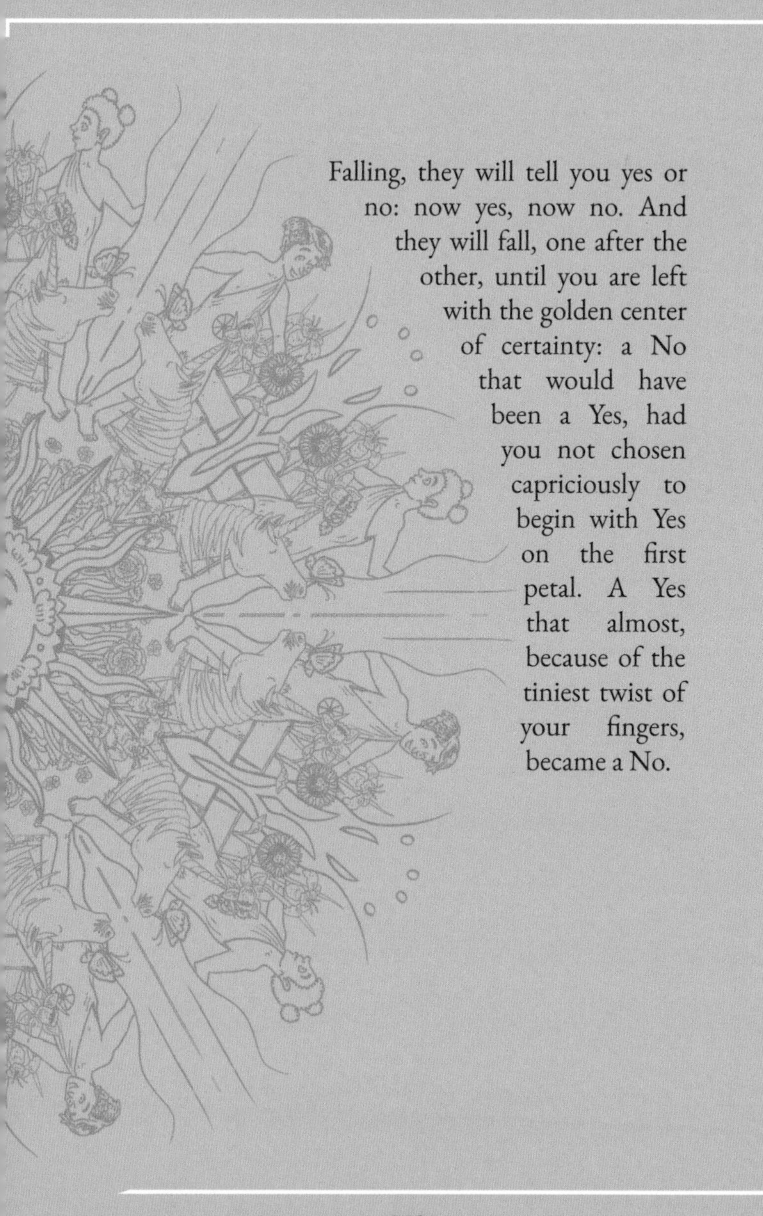

Falling, they will tell you yes or no: now yes, now no. And they will fall, one after the other, until you are left with the golden center of certainty: a No that would have been a Yes, had you not chosen capriciously to begin with Yes on the first petal. A Yes that almost, because of the tiniest twist of your fingers, became a No.

XX
JUDGMENT

•

I am the angel of Temperance, of integration. Without integration, temperance cannot last; without temperance, integration cannot be. Your distempered excesses will provoke confusion; only through a healthy discipline will you attain knowledge and complete a self that, never having left you, has seemed so far away.

Resurrection is the old fantasy about the meeting of body and soul. As the painter awakens the spirit in the pigment, the pigment allows the painter's spirit to be. The grinding of matter creates new matter. As you come to the end—almost the end—of your road, think: Have your steps taken you here, or have they taken you away from where you weren't?

The trumpet will bleat once again. Let me explain its sounds. The painters of old made four colors out of lead: brown, orange, yellow, and white. In earthenware jars, they oxidized the lead, exposing it to vinegar fumes, and they expedited the oxidation by sinking the jars in fermenting dung. The whiteness of this banner comes from the emanations of the foul.

When you think, as you inevitably will, of the decay of your body, think of the old painters. When your hair falls, your skin furrows, your teeth rot, your shank sags, and your eyes sink into the milk of darkness, think of my lesson, Magician. We all go to death, yes, we all blanch out into ashes and, as our names fade into the syllables of Babel and our salt longs for a return to the sea, let us remember that we sprang from excretion and have fed on the rot of death. We go to the earth's unforgiving sludge whence we come.

XXI
THE WORLD

•

I am the beauty of life and the life of beauty. I am the laurel of the garland that is the poet's prize. My four children—the tetramorphs: ox, lion, eagle, and man—bearers of my news, elements of my being, lend me equilibrium and harmony: the blue sky and the luminosity of a clear spring day, plants in bloom, compost in effervescence, the smell of earth back in the air, and cool water again desirable even as we light the last fires of the year. I am inevitable. I am ungraspable. I am effable. And as I unfold, I am incorrigible.

Or I am a story and, like any story, a repetition and a cycle, a return, perhaps a return to where we never were. The circular garland signifies that everything begins anew, and the tetramorphs that all knowledge is nothing more than narration of the facts. In the beginning was a fiction, and from that fiction we all come, spun from the tales of time and matter.

With me you have the certainty of having reached knowledge. You have reached movement and circularity, elements of wisdom: an unstable rest on a stony frieze of frenzy. You are there: this is it. This is it, as you see, even though it turns and appears more uneasy than ever, for I am also savage Kali's dance.

My card heralds total compenetration with wisdom, the understanding of truth beyond thought, and therefore the card is useless, because the wise need no confirmation of their wisdom, and neither do the fools.

THE TAROT *BETWEEN REASON AND FOLLY*

ABOUT THE TAROT

•

A traditional, participatory art of self-exploration through images, a playful relative of the Neoplatonic philosophies from which it derives or to which it relates, the Tarot is inevitably met at first with skepticism. How can a random shuffling of cards produce any truth about ultimate matters? How can a set of inanimate objects claim knowledge of anyone's psyche and even spirit? How could anyone learn anything from a game of cards? The most learned of arguments would be insufficient to satisfy questions of this kind and dispel such doubts; and in any case dislodging such doubts from one's reason might not amount to obliterating them. I propose instead that the readers set aside their skepticism, at least for the time of reading this book, and use it to question the information that follows.

Skepticism is a healthy initial response to the Tarot, yet a good reading of the cards normally produces a sense of awe that would shake the convictions of the most doubting of Thomases. Baffling experiences produced by the art of divination are anything but rare; many people have been amazed by the accuracy of the message in the cards. To begin our approach to the Tarot, then, let us place ourselves between skepticism and awe, and approach the cards with neither mistrust nor gullibility. Such an intellectual position, in which it does not matter what one believes, a position independent of credibility, the "suspension of disbelief" touted by literary critics, may be the ideal starting point for our examination of the Tarot.

Whatever its origins and ultimate essence, the Tarot is a system for self-exploration rooted in traditional, pre-scientific thought. The Tarot, like alchemy, is one of the human quests for the unattainable, and like alchemy it sprang during a period when Western thought was more static than it is today. The fact that our age has by and large abandoned such quests and developed a scientific method based on experimentation, however, should not make us turn our backs to that grand pursuit for a knowledge that transcends all human limitations, including reason.

Yet the Tarot is not necessarily irrational. Or is it as irrational as any artistic activity, as intuition, as mystic passion? The Tarot blends reason with the faith in the quest for an inner truth. It is related to other occult activities, particularly to astrology, numerology, and alchemy in so far as they are all rooted in complex, idealistic (Neoplatonic), un-experimental methods, and in so far as they have all enjoyed favor and disfavor from the institutions in power.

But it is my contention that the Tarot does not need to be shrouded in mystery. It was fashionable during the nineteenth century to dress the Tarot in the mumbo-jumbo of charlatanry, to turn down the lights, speak in whispers, wear robes, and be as befuddling as one would get away with. This mystique led to inflated claims about the power of the cards. The more obscure you were, the more you could pretend to divine the future and reveal the darkest secrets from the past. A rather repressed era was eager for big thrills.

Not everybody of course can become a good card reader, or even a passable one, by simply reading this book or any, or all, books on the subject. Like any other form of art, the Tarot takes a certain disposition, an openness, a flexibility—in short, talent. Like any other art, the Tarot will allow improvement with experience and practice.

HOW TO READ THE CARDS

•

The kind of tradition the Tarot has emerged from is based on the juxtaposition of ideas, on the combination of thoughts, on analogy. That tradition is idealistic; that is, it is based on principles rather than results, and those principles reveal themselves numerically.

Any card reading begins with the shuffling of the cards. Shuffling is an image of chaos, of the primordial confusion that precedes all realization, of the darkness that gives sense to light. The reading recreates the history of our notion of the universe, from chaos to order. The moment of shuffling is also an invitation to mediation. The cards are to be shuffled of course by the person to whom they are to be read. If you do this for a friend, let your friend shuffle, while you observe, and both concentrate. Other than in moments of ecstasy and sleep, we are always in this life dealing with some kind of issue or problem, and often with more than one. The shuffling is an invitation to bringing out into our awareness whatever preoccupation we are grappling with at present. Whether we have difficulties dealing with our spouse, whether things are not going well at work, whether we are unhappy for no specific reason—these are the kinds of issues the cards can help bring into focus. As we shuffle the pack, our minds begin to open to the possibilities the world at all times keeps in store for us. The practice of Tarot reading is thus eminently positive, optimistic; from this comes its immense popularity.

The shuffling itself is the initial meditation of the game. One method consists in dividing the pack into three piles and then shuffling each pile while concentrating or reflecting respectively on our body, our mind, and our spirit; then the cards are shuffled altogether in a final communion of the self.

This triple shuffling, a reminder of the traditional value of number three associated with the divinity in the many Trinitarian religions of the world, bows to the gods (I prefer the plural, lower case form of the word because here I do not espouse any particular religion). Then, after reassembling the cards, we may proceed to cutting the final pile into two. Cutting is a gesture of decision ('decide' comes from a root meaning 'to cut'), of separation, of clarification. It is the human process of curiosity, the beginning of the investigation. Cutting the pile is therefore a crucial step.

From this point on, the methods are many; most books on the Tarot explain one or several in detail, and the little pamphlets which come with Tarot packs normally offer appropriate guidelines. My comments here will be of a more general nature, as I leave the explanation, say, of the Celtic Cross or of Jacob's Ladder to further readings.

But I would suggest starting with number two. The inexperienced reader should not tackle a complex structure, but rather the simplest: two cards. And even one single card should provoke at least two readings. My oracles for the Lesser Secrets are therefore dual.

Start, then, with two cards, and consider one to be the true but hidden nature of the problem you are facing at the moment, and the other (which can be placed transversally over the first) as the apparent form of that problem. Say that you draw the Three of Clubs and the Eight of Golds. Say that the Three of Clubs symbolizes your deeper need to look ahead and chart your course, while the Eight of Golds signifies your present wealth, anchoring you in security. The juxtaposition of both cards will lead you to meditate that perhaps your present economic comfort is an impediment or deterrent to your looking ahead to an open, more adventurous future.

From this beginning you may branch out. Surround, for example, the two crossed cards with four others, placed at the cardinal points. Let us say that you have drawn the Three of Cups as North, the King of Swords as South, the Two of Clubs as East, and the Five of Cups as West. The Three of Cups, or disinterested fulfillment, is your goal, yet you are dragged down by the King of Swords, deceit or self-deceit; and meanwhile you are oscillating between the future-oriented optimism of the Two of Clubs, and the past-oriented pessimism of the Five of Cups.

The above simple spread of six cards, perhaps a little too balanced for comfort, draws a rather clear psychological portrait that you can easily color with your experiences and expectations. We have made so far numerical references to the duality of the human psyche (the cutting of the pack, the initial two cards), and to the trinity of the divine (the triple shuffling); we have also, with the following four cards, traced a cross, like the baptismal cross which is traced over the waters as a distant echo of the ancient belief in the separation of the waters, in the calling up of the four elements. Having done all this, you might want to draw one more card, and use it as a kind of key or solution to the conundrum between fear and hope that you had drawn and so as to have a total of seven cards, considering how traditionally magic the number seven is. Imagine, to continue with our hypothetical reading, that your seventh card is the Ace of Swords; you can easily see in it an invitation to action, and the power to topple the King of Swords. Instead of this last step you may want to draw a file of four new cards to one side, so as to have a total of ten, and imagine that those four cards make a story of relevance to your present situation.

A different kind of throw involves dividing the pack of cards into four piles, one for each suit (into five piles if playing with a Tarot deck with the Major Arcana), then shuffling each suit-pile, cutting, and selecting one card each from the suits of Clubs, Cups, Swords, and Golds, and then one from the Greater Secrets as a way out of the puzzlement of the other four. But for this method you need to be quite familiar with the general characteristics of the suits, about which you can read something later in this introduction.

Up to here I have illustrated sketchily two basic methods for card throwing. Try them, and try others. Try one first with regular playing cards, guided by the examples in this book. Be playful. Make a ladder which might represent a progression from where you are to where you want to be; make it a double ladder for the journey there and back. Or make a circle of cards with one or two in the middle. Always relate cards to one another, think of them in pairs, trios and quartets. Do it many times, do it for your spouse, your child, your friend. Soon you will be ready to choose your own pack.

CHOOSING A TAROT SET

•

During a recent visit to a bookstore, I counted eighteen different sets of Tarot cards displayed for sale. I own a modest collection of seven sets of which only one was represented in that store. I have no idea how many types of Tarots are presently available in the market; one company alone offers 31 "popular" Tarot decks, 20 facsimile decks, and 26 "others" in addition to some cartomancy decks. But take heart: for playing the game you only need one set. As a matter of fact it is best to have only one so you can study it time after time and grow with it.

There are a number of beliefs attached to Tarot sets: they should be kept wrapped in silk, nothing in the room should be stored higher than the cards, and other injunctions of this nature. They appear to my mind as a worship of the obscure, but they call attention to the simple fact that by surrounding your cards with some kind of ritual you will increase your enjoyment of the game. Again, you may want to develop your own approach and let your creativity dictate the rules. I have also heard that one should never purchase or even choose one's own set, but be given one selected by some friend or teacher. There is nothing wrong with waiting for that happy gift if you think it is going to happen soon. There is nothing wrong either with going ahead and acquiring one with your well-earned money. Let your choice be guided by your intuition. Play with this book and with an ordinary deck of cards first. Get other people to read the cards for you. See how your heart responds to the diverse decks they will surely be using. After you have gained enough experience, you will know.

The three most popular decks are, in their most common names, the *Marseilles*, the *Rider-Waite-Smith*, and the *Crowley* decks. I shall limit my discussion to those three, although by no means do I think my readers ought to limit their choices to them.

The *Marseilles* is the most traditional of all the commercially available decks. Its main characteristics are common to most decks, and make up the classic form of the cards: a series of 22 figure cards, called the Major Arcana or Greater Secrets, and four suits of 14 cards each: a total of 78 cards, then. The suits are *Batons* (Clubs), *Coupes* (Cups), *Épées* (Swords), and *Deniers* (Golds); each suit has ten number or pip cards and four figures or face cards: *Valet* (Page), *Cavalier* (Knight), *Roy* (King), and *Reine* (Queen). As this system reoccurs with minor variations in most other decks I shall discuss it in greater detail later on in this introduction.

The main difference between the *Marseilles* deck and the other two is that here the Lesser Secrets do not have descriptive designs but simply the stylized emblems of the suits, and the lesser figure cards are rather similar from suit to suit. This makes this deck difficult to read by the novice. The *Marseilles* deck dates back to the fourteenth century, however, and this is the oldest and most traditional of all available decks. It has also inspired a significant number of writings, including an illuminating essay by Joseph Campbell. The 22 Greater Secrets, on the other hand, are well distinct and constitute the iconographic source for most other Tarots, including the *Rider-Waite-Smith* deck.

The *Rider-Waite-Smith* deck is so called because it was first issued by the London publisher Rider; it is now sold by U.S. Games Systems, Inc. with a helpful booklet written by Stuart R. Kaplan and with excerpts from A.E. Waite's *Key to the Tarot*. The *Rider-Waite-Smith* deck was designed under the direction of this scholar of the occult, Arthur Edward Waite (1857-1942), by the American Pamela Colman Smith. Waite and Smith were members of the Order of the Golden Dawn, a group of students of symbolism related to the Rosicrucians. Other well-known members were Aleister Crowley, and the Irish poet and playwright William Butler Yeats.

The *Rider-Waite-Smith* deck dates from the first decade of the twentieth century and it derives much of its imagery from the symbolism studies of the Tarot undertaken during the eighteenth and nineteenth centuries. Each card, including the pip cards of the Lesser Secrets, has its own revealing design. Miss Smith was a stage designer who collaborated with Yeats. Her pictures for the cards have a theatrical quality with figures that look like actors on a stage; a stage, however, that ignores the limitations of indoor theaters, as it often presents mountains and bodies of water. Ultimately, Smith's designs offer visions that could well be in a dream. Hers is my favorite deck, the one I use, and the one that has inspired many of the examples in this book. Smith's visions, however, are not the mere inventions of hers or of Waite's; they reproduce in many cases historical designs from a number of sources, including alchemical illustrations and books of emblems as well as those reproduced in a key work on Tarot, Antoine Court de Gébelin's *Le monde primitif*. The *Rider-Waite-Smith* deck, then, is a modern interpretation of traditional symbols.

In comparison with the other two, we could term the *Crowley* deck post-modern. In general, the idea of the *Crowley* deck differs little from that of the *Rider-Waite-Smith* deck. Again, a student of the occult, Aleister Crowley (1875-1947), collaborated with a painter, Lady Freida Harris, to produce a deck rich in symbolism (particularly with many references to astrology) and with individual designs for each of its 80 cards. This deck has two extra cards as its users are given the option of three different cards for the major arcanum number I, the Magician. Whenever you use this deck, then, you must start by selecting one among its three Magicians. (In contrast, the present book, in so far as it is a deck, has only 74 cards for reasons explained below.)

Aleister Crowley was for some, a remarkable person who had an instrumental influence on occultism today, but for others, at best, a colorful guru of the occult and, at worst, a dangerous psychotic who likes to describe himself as "the Great Beast" while many of those associated with him met with violent deaths. The deck he helped design, however, can be easily separated from his personality; it happens, incidentally, to be the favorite of two friends of mine who produce beautiful readings from it and are far from being satanic.

Frieda Bloxam (1877-1962), married to Sir Percy Harris, considered herself obligated and encouraged, by her guardian angel, to create the most exquisite deck in her power. Harris's Tarot paintings were exhibited at the London Berkeley Galleries in July 1942, but the deck was not published until 1969 and, in its definitive edition, 1977. Its colors are heavier, darker, and also subtler in their contrasts than those of Smith's. Harris's designs are more symmetrical and daring in their combinations of pictorial elements than the cartoon-like Smiths. Someone has described the Harris deck as "surrealistic," an adjective that fits its artistic realization better than its contents which are laden with symbols derived from astrology and from a number of mystical traditions such as Apocalypse illumination.

The decks themselves are interesting objects to study. Many of them, in their accumulation of symbols, are a compendium of the story of Tarot. Other decks break with tradition and are inventive and intuitive. By profession and temperament, I am attracted to those that incorporate symbols from a number of spiritual traditions, thinking that the wisdom and errors of many will be more illuminating and rewarding that the genius of one. So, I of course favor traditional decks, and think that their complexity is an enticement to further investigation and developed learning of the cartomantic tradition.

THE CARDS, THEIR HISTORICAL ORIGINS

•

Studies on the subject of playing cards, even unrelated to what is often called "the occult," are notably absent from most libraries. Only recently has historical scholarship turned its interest to the unheroic, and scholars are beginning to study such things as games that had long been considered frivolous. As a result, we know little about the origin of playing cards and Tarots, and much that we know is entangled in the highly imaginative protestations of the occultists.

That cards became widespread in Europe towards the end of the 14th century comes close to being the consensus among card historians. We should also keep in mind two preliminary considerations: All of the authors I have been able to consult ignore the relationship between playing cards and the printing press or fail to take into consideration some form of mechanical reproduction of cards such as wood blocks; but surely the anonymity and unmarkedness that printing would ensure is necessary for playing cards. Another puzzle is the unexamined assumption of most card historians that the decks of cards were originated in basically the same format as we know today, even though those writers allow for the variations of the suit designs from one culture to another. Present-day cards from India and the Far East (which knew the press before Europe) are very different from our decks in design, organization, and number. Other games, such as the Game of the Goose (a predecessor of Monopoly), and board games, most notably chess, bear striking similarities to Tarot cards. The Bishop in chess is not unlike the Hierophant; there is also a King (the Emperor, in Tarot), a Queen (the Empress), a Rook or Castle (the Tower), a Knight (as in the Minor Arcana). Either cards derived from board games or both cards and boards share a common source for their imagery, perhaps related to the signs of the Zodiac if not to astrology itself. Surely the basic idea of the combination of archetypes has evolved variously.

The more traditional packs we have today must have congealed in the European early Renaissance; some Tarot notions are frequent topics in late medieval and renaissance literature and lore: the Fool, the Dance of Death, the Pope, the Tower struck by lightning, the Wheel of Fortune. In recent times there has been an outburst of interest in the Tarot with a remarkable renovation of the packs. We now have Aquarian Tarots, Native American Tarots, Cat People Tarots, Motherpeace rounds, and all kinds of packs drawing on different mythological traditions—with minor but real differences in the number and order of the cards. This modern multiplicity confirms my supposition that playfulness is the essential element in the cards and that any hypothesis that assumes the packs to have been fixed from antiquity is to be doubted. Even the three decks described above which follow quite closely the same tradition show significant variations.

One author, Hillel Schwartz, reflecting that the oldest Tarot pack we have, the Visconti-Sforza deck (reproduced in Dummett 1986 and datable to ca. 1450), shows already the traditional form we accept today, has claimed an Italian birthright for the whole Tarot. Michael Dummett would narrow it to fifteenth-century

Ferrara. In a recent article, Schwartz makes a very good case for the Italian origin of the cards, which in his opinion ultimately derive from ancient Roman triumphal processions adapted in due course by the medieval Church and transformed by Renaissance princes. Indeed, the etymology for 'trump' goes back to the Italian *triomfo*. Indeed, the Chariot (Greater Secret VII) goes back to ceremonious military and religious parades. Indeed, the Papess or High Priestess (II) may be Popess Joan, a popularization of the figure of Guglielma of Milan, who died in 1281. Indeed, the Hanged Man (XII) may be the representation of the way in which traitors were paraded in Italian victory processions. For the historian, the cards, ever a mirror for those who approach them, become pure history.

Oswald Wirth had seen the origins of Tarot imagery in the late Middle Ages. The two theories combined would discredit claims for more ancient origins. There might have been Tarot cards as far back as ancient Egypt; it is highly unlikely (and totally undocumented) that they would be very close to the forms we follow today.

There is some likelihood that the medieval playing cards were "occultized" from the seventeenth century onwards, and particularly by the eighteenth-century revival of interest in ancient Egypt, exemplified by the growth of the order of the Rosicrucians (created ca. 1615 but claiming a medieval origin) and in the rediscovery of alchemical and gnostic texts. Michael Dummett (1980) has made a case for this "occultization" (but see Frances Yate's review of his book). One of the classic works on the Tarot, perhaps the oldest extant, is found in volume eight of Antoine Court de Gébelin's encyclopedic work *Le monde primitif*. Court de Gébelin sees in the Tarot pack nothing less than the ancient book of the Egyptian Thoth. Court died shortly before the French Revolution; he was a Freemason (and a friend of Benjamin Franklin's); he may be said to be the first theoretician of Tarot and influenced the development of the learned interest in the cards; his sources, however, remain a mystery.

So do those for tracts on the discipline. Part of the game has been to assume a magical stance, a prophetic tone, an attitude verging on charlatanry. A certain obscurity and mystery are of course essential springboards for the kind of imagination needed for this game. For the Tarot is a game; a game, however, that may not be as frivolous as games are taken to be.

Another route to learning about the Tarot is the study of those concepts and activities associated with the cards. The etymologies of the names given to those associations may serve as a guide.

THE NAME TAROT

•

It has become traditional to associate the name Tarot with Thoth, although I suspect here an analogical attribution developed *a posteriori*. Thoth is the Egyptian lunar god, credited with the invention of writing and worshipped later as a demiurge by the Gnostics. Thoth is also the judge who weighed the souls, and the god of Magic. The Greeks assimilated Thoth to Hermes. From the name of this god come our words 'hermetic' and 'hermeticism,' and also 'hermit' (see the Greater Secret IX in the oracles). Tarot commentaries see this god as the first of the Greater Secrets, the Magician.

Some of the symbolism we find in Tarots indeed derives from works attributed to Hermes. The *Corpus Hermeticum* is the title given to a collection of writings on alchemy (Scott), including the *Precepts of Hermes Trismegistus* or Thrice-Greatest Hermes, a Greek adaptation of the Egyptian Thoth from the early Christian era. The Greek's indebtedness to the Egyptians has been recently emphasized by Martin Bernal's revolutionary book *Black Athena*, but our sources for the origins of alchemy come from medieval Arabic texts, including the just-mentioned *Precepts*, also called *Tabula Smaragdina* (a recent English translation can be found in Luck 370) as they were supposedly written on an emerald tablet.

The word 'alchemy' derives through Arabic from a probably Egyptian word, *kamt* or *quemt* (preceded by the Arabic article *al*) which seems to refer to the black silt of the Nile, the life-giving substance of Egyptian economy; from the Arabic *alkimya* come our words 'alchemy' and 'chemistry'. Alchemy, the forerunner of chemistry, presents a practical side devoted to the transmutation of metals, and a mystical side. The latter, consisting of a quest for spiritual perfection, has many points in contact with Tarot symbolism, as I hope to make apparent when I discuss individual cards later in this essay. The alchemists' notion of water as the element from which everything springs out and to which all transformation must recur must have exerted a strong influence on Waite and Smith; the characters in their designs often stand near or upon some body of water. Other alchemical symbols occur in many cards, one of them being the *ouroboros* or serpent that eats itself (see the ancient text and illustration in Luck). Whether these symbols from the alchemists were originally in the Tarot, or were added to its designs during the eighteenth and nineteenth centuries, the present scholarship, as far as I know, cannot tell. But it is undeniable that both alchemy and the Tarot have had their impact on the modern psychology of the unconscious.

In spite of all this, no etymologist would trace the word Tarot to Thoth. It is undeniable, however, that somehow Tarot relates, or has been made to relate, to a very ancient psychological tradition. While scientific thinking is based on relations of cause and effect, the kind of thinking we could call magical is based on correspondences or sympathies. At the base of all magical beliefs is the notion that the universe is tightly interconnected, and that nothing gratuitous happens in it. This is, incidentally, a belief today's scientists are beginning to admit to. Would this include thought and fantasy? The magical approach to reality is a kind of reading of the universe—or of a part of it, like the system of Tarots. What brings together the cards and the Egyptian Hermes is analogy rather than causality.

An ingenious analogy relates the word Tarot to the Latin word *rota*—'the wheel'—as this word is read in the form of a wheel: roTA-ROTa-rota... Often the tenth of the Greater Secrets shows these letters drawn on the wheel, and one reads them clockwise:

T
O A
R

Read counterclockwise, the anagram reads 'Tora.' (The final 'h' sometimes appended to English spellings of this word does not occur in Hebrew.) The Tora is the main body of Jewish religious literature, a name that stands for the Book. In considering the Tarot as a learning tool, the analogy becomes more vivid. In some modern representations, the second of the Major Arcana, the High Priestess, holds a document titled Tora on her lap.

One more reading of the anagram gives the Catalan word *orat*. The word means 'fool' and for its interpretation I must refer to later commentaries about the unnumbered arcanum and to the oracle for that card.

We can begin to see that whatever we are dealing with, and however we feel or think about it, the Tarot forms a flexible system, an open, playful system. It invites the mind to move along in many ways, from mere mechanical reorganizations of the cards to mystical flights of eschatology. The Tarot is a porous construction that can assimilate all kinds of significations.

OTHER ETYMOLOGIES

•

I use the word 'oracle' to refer to the examples in this book. *Webster's New International Dictionary of the English Language* (Harris) defines the word, principally, as "the medium by which a god reveals hidden knowledge or makes known the divine purpose; also the place where the oracle is given." 'Oracle' derives from Latin *oraculum*, a word related to *orare*, 'to speak' or, in other words, 'to use one's mouth.' *Orare* comes from *os, oris* ('the mouth')—the root of this whole family of words. In Latin, as in English, *oraculum* could also refer to the sayer of the oracle, to the person who becomes the mouth of the gods. Not very far, I should think, from what a poet is. Or a prophet; 'prophet' derives from the Greek *prophetes*, 'a person who speaks for someone else.' The oracle or speaker for the god is then the 'diviner', and divination is one of the attributes of the cards.

The Catalan word *orat* is related in sound to *oracle* but not in etymology. *Orat* means 'fool', and even though etymologists derive it from *aura*, 'wind,' it nevertheless brings to the notion of the oracle the figure of the unnumbered major arcanum, the Fool. The Fool is an echo of the first major arcanum, the Magician, so I have let my peroration bring together Magician, Poet, and Fool. The Joker and Juggler should be added to this, as we shall see in a moment.

Just as we read the word Tarot in a circle, there is, in Magician and Fool, a coincidence of first and last. The same coincidence appears throughout any game of cards; a good example is the ambivalence of the lowest number in each suit which may be considered a lowly one or a sovereign ace. So the association of Tarot to *rota* makes good sense. Etymologists, however, disregard it, claiming that the Italian word for Tarot, *tarocco*, is the oldest documented word to refer to the cards and cannot be read circularly. The first recorded use of "Tarocchi" (plural of *tarocco*) is found in one of the account books of the court of Ferrara for 1516. I cannot argue against this evidence although from the viewpoint of this book I am no one to disdain coincidence. This is precisely what we do when we play: we juggle and coincide. Let us not be surprised, then, to see the word Tarot, once we eliminate the duplication of the t, reads *orat* in reverse.

Oracles are, in any case, the proper activity of poets and orators: mouthers. A religious dimension is never far from poetry, even though in English the only etymological relation might be in the uncommon word 'orison.' A humbler word related to poet is 'jongleur,' akin to 'juggler.' In the Middle Ages, jongleurs were itinerant reciters or singers of poetry as well as entertainers. Etymologically, jongleur is the *joculator* or 'player'. We of course *play* cards. The jongleurs or jugglers partake in their names of the Indo-European root *yek*, from whence Latin *jocus* (a verbal game, that is, a joke) and all the forms in Romance, from Catalan and Spanish *jugar* to Italian *gioconda*, that convey the meanings of 'play.' But the root *yek* means 'to speak.' For to speak (or to orate) and to make poetry is always a little to play, and to play is always a little to deceive. In this manner the Poet and the Jongleur may become one with the Magician, and the Magician with the *orat* or Fool. Translated in psychological terms this coincidence of terms suggests that the key to one's higher nature has to be rooted on the acceptance of one's lower nature; no poet exists that has not embraced the fool of his or her self. The coincidence between some attributes of the first and the last of the Major Arcana, between Poet and Fool, could explain the existence in our decks of two cards called "jokers." One may easily suspect that they are the fossilized remnants of those two arcana, as the meaning of the name makes clear.

Another name given to playing cards is the Catalan *naip* and Spanish *naipe*. The Catalan form, which used to be pronounced in two syllables, naïp, appears in a document dated 1371. It is the oldest European allusion to playing cards. (See the entry "Naip," written by Joseph Gulsoy, in the Catalan etymological dictionary of Joan Coromines.) According to Gulsoy, the word could derive from the French *naïf*, meaning a person with little discernment. The word *naip*, being applied to cards in general, would underscore the importance of the Fool, which could be seen as the archetype of all cards, if we consider that 'folly' is a form of simplicity or naivete. The word 'card' comes from the Italian *carta* which means paper. Early Spanish documents (Ciruelo) inevitably refer to playing cards as *cartas de naypes*—that is, pieces of paper showing the Fool or Naif and his cohorts.

Nowadays we may uneasily relate folly to simplicity or 'nicety,' but it was current in medieval imagery. Etymology lends some support to the relationship as well. The usual word in French Tarots to signify Fool is *mat: le Mat*. Early Italian sources invariably call it *il Matto*. These forms approach the sound of the word 'magus' as well as that of 'mad.' The word *mat* given to that 'arcanum' derives from vulgar Latin *mattus*, which meant 'stupid' or 'brutish.' (See the entry *matar* in Coromines.) Oswald Wirth claims for these cards a medieval origin; his theory would justify my equation of the word for cards, *naips*, with the Fool.

The word Magus or Magician (*Mag*, in Catalan), a synonym of *oraculum*, is another of the names given to the major arcanum number I. The word derives, through Irani, from the Indo-European root *magh*, which means 'power' or 'to have power.' Curious etymological relatives of this word are 'Mathilde' (a woman's given name), 'machine,' and, with a negative prefix, 'dismay' (i.e., loss of power). 'Magician,' then, is not a very different word from 'poet', which comes from the Greek *poiein*, meaning 'to make,' 'to create.' In Latin the word *vates* had the double meaning of prophet (or diviner) and poet. *Vates* derives from the Indo-European root *wat* which has given us the archaic English word 'wood' meaning someone violently crazy, a madman; the same root names the Germanic god Wotan or Woden. Again, the Fool lurks under the Poet; both bespeak the god.

THE LESSER SECRETS

•

Tarot packs total 78 cards divided into two groups called 'arcana' ('arcanum' in singular). This word (from Indo-European *arek*, 'hold,' 'guard') was dear to the cultivators of the mists of esotericism in card-reading, it means something like 'secret.' ('Arcanum' may be related to the Greek word *archai* which was used by the Gnostics to denote their principles.) We have, then, Major and Minor Arcana: the Greater and the Lesser Secrets.

The Minor Arcana are not essentially different from regular playing cards, although in modern versions they have taken elaborate and unique designs. These cards are distributed in four suits that correspond to the suits of European playing cards.

PACKS:					
Tarot	German	French	English	Spanish	Italian
SUITS:					
wand	Grün	trèfle	club	basto	bastone
cup	Herz	coeur	heart	copa	coppa
sword	Schelle	pique	spade	espada	spada
pentacle	Eichel	carreau	diamond	oro	denaro

Our modern cards derive from ancient ones that present-day Tarots reproduce with varying degrees of fidelity. In Spain and Italy, people continue to use traditional playing cards with the four suits: *Bastos* (Clubs), *Copas* (Cups), *Espadas* (Swords), and *Oros* (Golds). The design of the cards used internationally to play poker, bridge, canasta, and so on, suggests a French origin, but the names of the suits in English come close to the Spanish: 'spade' is a phonetic adaptation of 'espada' and 'club' is a lexical adaptation of 'basto.' The Spanish pack, as some scholars believe, may be a prototype of the European ones. (The German words in the table above mean, in the order given, 'leaf,' 'heart,' 'bell' and 'acorn'.) Otherwise, the differences between all these packs are few: the Spanish pack has no tens or Queens; the French has no Knights. All the packs have suffered transformations, owing to the historical vicissitudes of playing cards, but basically each suit consists of seven to ten number cards, called pip cards, and three or four figure cards, also called face cards.

In Europe there is no evidence for playing cards older than the late Middle Ages, the game of dice being known since Graeco-Roman times, and board games since at least the New Kingdom in Ancient Egypt (Dilke 53-56). A certain medieval lore accompanies the kind of game I am playing in this project. As I took to preparing my oracles, I immediately thought of the terminology traditional in my country: *Bastos, Copas, Espadas, Oros*. My oracular and jocular project began with a meditation over the meaning of those four emblems which relate to the seasons of the year.

Bastos or clubs are the only natural product among the four suits. For this reason, and because they take the form of wands that sprout, they must be related to spring. Spring is traditionally the season of incipient love. Being phallic symbols, the clubs represent the male sexual drive, if not love. They correspond to the trefoil in the poker deck (clearly a springtime emblem) which combines both aspects of the emblem (the wand and its sprouting) in the clover design and in its name 'club.'

Copas or cups—chalices that hold the liquid to assuage our thirst—correspond to summer. Cups associate themselves to the female where Clubs did to the male; in my examples, therefore, the face cards for this suit and for Golds culminate with the Queen. The image of quenching one's thirst is inseparable from the sentimental connotations that befit the canicular season. There must be some recognition of the sentimental content of the cup as emblem in the gospels: "Take away from me this chalice." This emotional content of the chalice explains the transformation of the emblem from a cup to a heart in the poker deck. In the seasonal distribution of literary genres that Northrop Frye presented in his *Anatomy of Criticism*, summer is the season corresponding to the genre of romance, while spring has its comedy, fall its tragedy, and winter its satire. In this vein we could also allot a primordial content to each suit: Clubs speak of physical strength, sexual desire and matters related to health; Cups tell of relationships and sentimental entanglements.

Espadas or Swords, then, would speak of the other power: political, military, factitious. According to Frye, autumn is the season related to tragedy, as it moves from the life of summer to the death of winter; it is the passage from a certain order—a sentimental flowering, let us say—to chaos or disorder. The sword symbolizes death and suffering as well as strength. In the modern packs, the swords have been stylized into spades which in French are called "piques." *Pique*, 'pike', is a metonym for 'sword'; the word in English recalls the Spanish *espada* from which it clearly derives.

Oros or golds signify gold pieces, money. Golds represent wealth—not the real wealth of the fruits of the earth, but acquired wealth, wealth of exchange. Because we are talking about acquired, kept wealth, I relate Golds with winter which is the time of year during which human life relies mostly on savings. In the French-type decks, the gold coins have been stylized as the rhombs that represent *Carreaux* or Diamonds, symbols of wealth. In the more illustrated Tarots they are again coins. In some of these the coins have a design of a five-pointed star called a pentacle. Traditionally, this is the star to denote humanity: it looks like the emblematic outline of a human figure stretched within a circle, with its head and limbs as its five tips. It is called the star of the Microcosm. In the Catholic tradition, the five-pointed star refers to the Virgin Mary, born of humans, as she is differentiated from God, referred to by the six-pointed star made out of two superimposed equilateral triangles. The six-pointed star is that of the Macrocosm. The pentacle is also the emblem of the Magician. The five-pointed star, then, symbolizes the culmination of the human potential that the Church sees in the Virgin, and cartomancy, *mutatis mutandis*, in the Magician.

Having reflected on the general meaning of the four suits, I devoted one season of the year to each suit. There are thirteen weeks per season, and it seemed only natural to give one card to each week. But the Spanish pack that I followed had only twelve cards per suit, which left me four weeks short of the year. So, having one free week per season and finding it logical and licit to add one card per suit, I adapted to the Spanish pack a card that appears in the other systems: the Queen, which for some reason had been excluded from the Spanish deck. Such decks have the three figure cards of *Sota* or Page, *Caballo* or Knight, and *Rey* or King; the addition of a *Reina* compensated somewhat the absence of a feminine figure since a lamentable phallocentrism, disguised as prudery, had beheaded the Spanish deck. I have also tried to combine male and female characteristics in my Pages and Knights.

Just as there is a progression in each suit, from the mandala-like intuition of the ace to the full human realization of the King or Queen, there is also a progression of the suits. The Clubs stand for the most physical aspects of humanity; through love and feeling, the Cups signal the passage into the emotional and therefore the beginning of the spiritual; the Swords speak of battle, that is, of transcendent enterprises and the heroic quest; Golds stand for illumination, for finding the divine in one. For the alchemists too, gold was not just the symbol but also the substance of divine illumination and the object of the highest quest. The alchemical progression of the suits is echoed in the frequent presence of the Tetramorphs in several of the cards (see for one example the Wheel of Fortune); a relationship could be drawn between Clubs and the Ox, Cups and the Lion, Swords and the human-looking Angel, and Golds and the divine Eagle. Another assimilation would be with the four functions of consciousness of Jungian psychology: intuition (Clubs), sensation (Cups), feeling (Swords), and thinking (Golds). Quaternary principles are abundant and essential. The above neat progressions, however, are disregarded in the shuffling of the cards, a fact which in itself is a warning against the tyranny of intentionality. The author too recommends separating the intellectual ordering of the system from the practical experiencing of the readings. The game itself suggests as essential rotation. The suits follow each other like the seasons in the year, eventually returning to the starting point, just like the wheel of time: Rota/Tarot.

The references to a number of disciplines I have just explained will make clear the importance of number four and will root the playing cards in traditional religious thought. The cross traced over baptismal waters, for example, divides them into four. The Tetramorphs are related to the four Evangelists, that is to the complete knowledge of the word of God. Alchemists too spoke of four elements: earth, air, water, and fire—and gold is found in the earth, cups may hold water, swords cut the air, and the wood of clubs feeds the fire. A four-fold system is one of balance and completion. In the four suits, we may easily see a grid for the human personality, a grammar of the conscious life to be transcended and completed by the Major Arcana.

THE GREATER SECRETS

•

The Greater Secrets or Major Arcana consist of 22 cards outside of the four-suit system. These are the most famous Tarots, and have inspired a hefty literature. While the Minor Tarots suggest a wheel, the Major Arcana suggest a development, a road, the progression of spiritual growth. Being numbered and outside of the system of suits speaks in favor of their linearity.

Many authors (see for example the Tarot entries in J. E. Cirlot's *Dictionary of Symbols*) advise the integration of a random, lunar approach with a solar and methodical—seasonal—approach such as I have used with the four suits. Yet I developed a logic for the Greater Secrets also. Such logic rests upon, or resounds against, some theories about psychological characterization in dream and theater. These theories are of course indebted to the archetypal approach to psychology developed by C. G. Jung. Jungian psychology explains the human psyche as made up of a series of elements (the animus, the anima, the shadow, and so on) that undoubtedly relate to the collective principles Jungians call "archetypes"; the psyche is a self-regulating system expressing itself in the process of individuation.

Jung's system of categories, his general notion of the complexity of the human soul, is one of the most comprehensive psychological theories. If we accept it, no matter how guardedly, we shall easily see the 22 Major Arcana as a kind of grammar of the psyche, a compendium of the possible forms it may take, or the archetypes it may follow.

The Major Arcana, then, may be seen as the various representations of the self, of the human psyche. Like psychological archetypes, like the forms in dreams and the characters in theater, the 22 Major Arcana are at once I and not-I, at once inside and out of the psyche. They represent, then, 22 milestones or clusters of possibilities for the self: the 22 cases of our psychic declension. A certain ambivalence impregnates the examples I have written for the Greater Secrets. There, I am at once reader and read, author and audience, self and other. I speak the card and the card speaks me. And the card also speaks each reader as the readers speak themselves in each card.

These Greater Secrets also trace a road, the path of experience. An explorer follows the road; the traveling defines the road as such. The explorer has at the onset no personality; he (I identify with the explorer and thus make him masculine) is the receptacle of the personalities offered him, flesh for the masks that he is going to try on. The explorer is me, the author of those pages, as much as you, their reader. Along that road we will both experience life through the explorer who is, himself, our experience.

The road, which is the life-road of a person, shows four distinct legs (four ages perhaps) with an introduction and a conclusion. The arcanum without number, the Fool, and the first arcanum, the Magician, are the characters or the two aspects of the character that will undertake the journey. Some authorities claim the Fool to be the point of the departure for the growth process, and the Magician that of arrival; for others, the Fool's lack of self-consciousness, his or her selflessness, gives this character transcendence. I have come to see the Fool as an image of the person who has not come to terms with his or her psyche: a naïf who ignores the process of individuation, a person whose illusions have not been shattered by the recognition of the unconscious. Yet the Fool is not without his greatness.

Seeing the road of the Greater Secrets as a path towards the creation of what Paracelsus called the *homo maior*, or Jung the process of individuation, it is hardly surprising that most of its figures, with the notable exception of the Lovers (although in some Tarots this card is simply the Lover), stand in splendid isolation, each figure a lonely answer to the question "Who am I?". The first and most flexible of these figures is the Magician. This explorer goes under several names. The *Marseilles Tarot* calls him *Le Bateleur*, 'puppeteer'; likewise in Italian packs he is *Il Bagatto*. He is the Poet and the Magician, at once an artist and an imposter, the paradigm of the actor. He is the figure to manufacture significations and at the same time receive all the significations to follow. He is the key arcanum for the whole game. In the explanation that follows I use the word 'explorer' in order to underline that the card has a passive value, a receptive value, as much as an active one.

First leg: towards equilibrium or recognition of the self. During the first leg of the road, the explorer meets four characters. These, and all the others, are not always the same or presented in the same order in the different decks. In the sequence adopted here they are: The High Priestess (II), the Empress (III), the Emperor (IV), and the Hierophant (V). The High Priestess is also called the Papess in a number of decks; the Hierophant (a word meaning 'he who shows the sacred') can also be identified with a Papal figure. These two men and two women, two religious and two secular authorities, form the square: equilibrium. They represent, respectively, four attributes that the explorer might want to make his own: intuition, love, power, and science. Over (or under) these significations one may find others, particularly if we relate them to the four signs of the suits: clubs, cups, swords, and golds. The explorer (I) approaches four cards: he lives the experience of the four seasons. He also finds himself at point five; he has completed his human career in the form of the five-pronged star of the Microcosm.

Second leg: experience. If the first leg of the journey was that of the characters, the second is that of the adventures. We have not yet left the human sphere and thus the explorer will encounter five cards or tests. The first one, the Lovers (VI), signifies coupling or copulation, the establishment of a union of two equals. The second, the Chariot (VII), represents travel, the most usual and real metaphor for the learning process; it occupies the preeminent magic number: seven. Then come Fortitude (VIII) or the test in the face of adversity, the Hermit (IX) or experience, and, to close the cycle, Fortune (X), representing a review of all possibilities. We have thus reached the number ten, a suggestion of worldly perfection.

Third leg: judgment and its consequences. Some systems, such as the one presented in Cirlot's *Dictionary of Symbols*, consider the eighth secret to be Justice rather than Fortitude; Justice, however, fits better as the opener of the third leg of the journey which has to do with discernment and maturity: judgment. Thus Justice (XI) reminds us that any decision carries its consequences; the Hanged Man (XII) alludes to bad judgment; Death (XIII, the unlucky number) to destruction or to the disastrous results of judgment; and Temperance (XIV) to good results and the vivifying process of change and growth. As a consequence of judgment, a Dantesque process ensues, with a descent into hell, the Devil (XV), and a kind of purgatory, the Tower Struck by Lightning (XVI). Let us note that arcanum XV is the reversal of VI, the Lovers, and that XVI is the reversal of X, Fortune. In these two, the Devil and the Tower, the earlier emblems find their echo.

Two notes: Let me not speak lightly of bad judgment. The Tarot is anything but dogmatic. I hear the message of the Hanged Man not so much as one of equivocation but one of exploration through the unusual: judgment subjected to an upside-down perspective. Three feminine figures have appeared so far: Fortitude, Justice, Temperance, corresponding to three of the four cardinal virtues of Christianity. But where in the Tarot is the fourth and first in order, Prudence? I hear Prudence's cautious message in the words of the High Priestess (II).

Fourth leg: enlightenment. His personality all shaped, after experience and judgment, the explorer is ready for the fourth leg, which corresponds to Dante's Paradise or, at any rate, to processes of illumination: The Star (XVII) represents inspiration; the Moon (XVIII), reflected light, means apprenticeship through copy or imitation; and the Sun (XIX), direct light, represents unmediated science. A second phase in this leg is made up of the two action cards: Judgment (XX), referring to the power to change, and the World (XXI), suggesting a total power, and absolute dominion that will lead again to the ironic response in the unnumbered arcanum: the Fool.

The above formulation follows a number of traditional interpretations of the Major Arcana; what in it is my own and what I owe, after several years of avid reading, is no longer clear in my mind. Here too I have become a medium. I hope that my essay nevertheless conveys a fairly accurate idea of the whole process of human growth or experience as it relates to a series of characters. The cards, whatever other values they may have, represent a hierarchization of psychological archetypes.

In giving mouth to the Minor Arcana I took, so to speak, an official attitude of ambivalence, deciding on a straight and a reversed reading for each one—an oracle and a vision. Thus each card generated two messages that are not exactly contraries but rather two poles in between which readers may place their chosen interpretations. Such polarity is quite traditional in cartomancy; it is also an expression of the duality of nature. In a way, duality is a kind of safety valve, a help for the reader to adapt to circumstances, to take into account the many situations in human experience. It may be a deceit, but such a deceit has its reasons.

In Goethe's poem, the Earth Spirit says to Faust:

> In the floods of life, in the storm of work
> in ebb and flow,
> in warp and weft,
> cradle and grave,
> an eternal sea,
> a changing patchwork,
> a glowing life,
> at the whirring loom of Time I weave
> the living clothes of the Deity. (p. 23)

Yet the Major Arcana have transcended such a duality in their very own ambiguous humanity. Most of the Greater Secrets have become voices that express themselves in the first person. Some of them are silent, and we learn about them through the Magician's words as read from his diary. I do not mean to imply that those cards are silent by nature, that those concrete arcana are voiceless. I needed to convey to the reader that the individual characters in these cards exist as they are heard by the Magician. The Magician, an archetype of all audiences, brings them to life when he encounters them, so they all exist in his mind (which may well be also my mind and my reader's) as much as anywhere else. The first person, say, of the Empress could have been read in the third person of the diary, just as the third person of the Wheel of Fortune could have been told to us in a direct first person.

A HYPOTHESIS FOR THE TAROT

•

The above commentary suggests how the Tarot works for people: the cards put us in touch with our psychological makeup through the power of some primordial images that we somehow come to recognize from the storehouse of all those intangible realities we call 'the mind.' The linguist Noam Chomsky has spoken about an innate sense of language that precedes all grammars—we learn to speak by recognizing our innate, deep structure of language. In the same way, we recognize ourselves in the different archetypes of the Tarot. The Tarot, then, is a porous system that is eminently open to new significations. The system is based on images rather than ideas so that its grip on the user stems from a deeper level of participation. The Tarot works as a psychological tool and therefore attracts great interest, as nothing draws us more than the examination of our selves.

Here lies, therefore, the divinatory power of the cards. Being archetypes, they allow themselves to be worn by just about anyone; each card makes sense for everyone. But all the cards at once would create a cacophony of psychological images—for this reason, the shuffling, cutting and selecting becomes necessary. Our humanity means our partiality. In spite of a widespread slogan, we cannot be all we can be, because humans do not exist in isolation. Just as a tree needs its roots, we need to feed from the world. Just as a flower looks for light, we bend in the nourishing directions offered us. The Tarot recognizes the naiveté of the notion of individuality. We feed on our circumstances and are shaped by them. Our potential floats on the waves of chance.

The question nevertheless still persists: how can a random shuffling of the cards know anything about our circumstances? Perhaps the best answer for that would be to throw the cards and let them speak with their appropriateness. We may also reflect on the nature of randomness, which is just as implausible as that of coincidence. The Tarot certainly operates outside of the scientific mind. For all the efforts of the Jungians, the question of coincidence remains alien to science, and it would be foolish to attempt to prove otherwise—at least for the time being. Great scientists recognize the power of intuition, another form of unscientific coincidence, and more and more, the unexpected becomes part of their world—they stop searching in order to find.

The Tarot is no theory; my notes here certainly do not attempt to make it one, but simply to make it somewhat more explicit to the rational side of my mind. As a system of thought, the Tarot approaches the kind of thinking that gave birth to the avatars of Hinduism or to the ambiguities of Taoism; some authors are convinced that the cards came to us from India or China. Who knows...At any rate, being alternatives, the cards have attracted minds that are uncomfortable pacing the main road: mystics as well as agnostics, outcasts as well as eccentrics, antiquarians and futurologists, poets and charlatans, feminists and folklorists—groups as varied as the colors on the Magician's or the Fool's motley coat.

If philosophy is the love of wisdom, the cards' philosophy would start with its doubts about an absolute Wisdom, a coherent and unattainable Sophia, and would refuse to grant it their monogamous love. This is at least my understanding. The cards invite playfulness, dilettantism, polygamy, and license if not licentiousness; the wisdom of the cards is as open and undefined as our existence in this world. The cards recognize all wisdom to be relative and, even more, that the knowledge we may attain is at best a happy coupling of images and life. The voices in the cards may help us hear some of the many voices we carry inside. And of course, even this is ciphered by a Magician who could well be a swindler, or a Fool. The wealth of the cards lies in how little they really promise: a game of chance, a turn of fate, but with it a flexibility and a vivacity that the brainiest of scientists could never reach.

OBITUARY JOSEP MIQUEL (PEP) SOBRER, SEPT. 2, 1944 – JAN. 1, 2015

•

Pep died of complications from metastatic colon cancer. As was his wish, he died at home, peacefully, and donated his body to the IU Anatomical Education Program. The following obituary, with some minor tweaking, was written by Pep in October of 2014:

Josep Miquel (Pep) Sobrer Barea was born in 1944 in Barcelona, the son of Gonçalo Sobré Travesset and Antònia Barea Mallorques, and brother of Gonçal Sobrer Barea. Pep graduated from the Universitat de Barcelona in 1967 and then moved to Eugene, Oregon, to study Romance Languages and Literatures earning a Ph.D. at the University of Oregon in 1972. Since then, he held several academic jobs, at the University of Puget Sound, at the University of Michigan, and finally at Indiana University, where he retired as professor emeritus in 2009. He was married three times, to Judith Berg Sobré, to Frances Wyers, and, getting it right finally, to Francesca Schmertz Sobrer with whom he had a son, Miró Henry Sobrer and two stepchildren, Greer and Ryland McIntyre.

In essence, the ten lines above are the skeleton of Pep's life; the muscles, tendons, nerves, and organs are less easy to summarize. He tried to squeeze as much out of life as his personality's tendencies to moroseness and pessimism allowed. He loved literature and the arts in general—his brother is a talented painter and his son a devoted musician; both relations delighted Pep. He loved writing and would have been accomplished in the craft if it weren't for a number of chronic conditions such as laziness and insecurity, and the fact that he could not decide which of his three main languages—his native Catalan, his adopted English, and the Spanish of his early schooling—he should concentrate on.

Pep was much admired and respected as an academic—at IU, he taught Spanish and Catalan literature; chaired the Spanish, Portuguese and Catalan Department for many years of his tenure. In his native Catalan, he was the editor of *Catalan Review* and was well known for his numerous translations of essays, books, and poetry. Pep was also a columnist for *The Herald-Times*, writing witty observations on life. He most enjoyed translating poetry. Pep was happy about some of the books he published, as he was unhappy about some others—and at times, about the same ones. If any of the good friends reading this would be moved to read something by Pep, he'd recommend, in English, *The Book of Oracles* and, in Catalan, *Desfer les Amèriques*.

He found some things difficult in this life: reading verbosity, telling people what to do, speaking on the phone (except when he was courting his dear Francesca), Indiana winters, and, increasingly, sleeping through the night. He loved family and friends as much as he was capable of. He also loved being on or by a river, climbing a mountain, sailing on a ferry boat, bad jokes, puns of any sort, rhyming poetry, playing tennis (he was a notable double-faulter), coffee, and a good dinner party.

At this moment in his obituary, Pep would feel it was already too long and would suspect only the most obsessive types would want to continue reading. At the same time, he would say that no life could be summarized verily without mention of some of the sinews of the deceased personality: failures and hatreds among them. Pep was ready to think his work a failure and, conversely, detested those who boasted of their successes. He couldn't stand people who complained, much less those who thought that "How are you?" is actually a question. He hated being shoved in the face with the religious beliefs of others. A devout atheist, he felt that those who invoke a god are, in essence, power seekers. He also loathed the laic form of religion that is patriotism and militarism, and felt particular disdain for politicians who draped their very self-serving interests with the flag of country and the name of God—most politicians, in fact. Less intensely, he despised writers who felt no sympathy for their characters, no matter how misguided or evil.

But Pep is dead, now. He would think that all this doesn't matter, and that the world will continue to stumble on until it bursts, hopefully long in the future. Pep had difficulty admiring historical personages, as he thought his admiration would serve no purpose. He felt, nevertheless, an affinity with several fictional characters (Cassandra from Greek myth among them), and would like, from the grave, to send his thanks to those who loved him, and to the writers who made him laugh, among them Nabokov, Cervantes, S. J. Perelman, Wodehouse, and in general to all those, artists mostly, who have endeavored to give people honest entertainment. If any of Pep's work would qualify as a product genuinely appreciated, he would be most happy—except for the fact that he is dead. Surely Pep would add a final thanks to those who have read or listened to this obituary.

WORKS CITED

•

Bernal, Martin. *Black Athena; The Afro-Asiatic Roots of Classical Civilization*. New Brunswick: Rutgers University Press, 1987.

Burckhardt, Titus. *Alchemy*. Longmead, Shaftesbury, Dorset: Element Books. 1967.

Campbell, Joseph, and Richard Roberts. *Tarot Revelations*. 3rd. ed. San Anselmo, CA: Vernal Equinox Press, 1987.

Chomsky, Noam. Cartesian linguistics; a Chapter in the history of Rationalist Thought. 1st ed. New York: Harper & Row, 1966.

Cirlot, J[uan] E[duardo]. *A Dictionary of Symbols*, 2nd ed. Jack Sage, trans. New York: Philosophical Library, 1971.

Ciruelo, Pedro. *Tratado en el qual se reprueban todas las supersticiones y hechizerias.* Barcelona, 1628. Facsimile edition: Puebla (Mexico): Universidad Autónoma, 1986.

Coromines, Joan, ed. *Diccionari etimològic i complementari de la llengua catalana*. 14 vols. Barcelona: Curial, 1980-1988.

Court de Gébelin, Antoine. "Du Jeu des Tarots," in Vol. 8 of his *Le Monde primitif, analysé et comparé avec le monde moderne*. Paris: Author's printing, 1781.

Dilke, O. A. W. *Mathematics and Measurement*. London: British Museum Publications, 1987.

Dummett, Michael. *The Game of Tarot from Ferrara to Salt Lake City*. (With Sylvia Mann.) London: Duckworth, 1980.

Dummett, Michael. *The Visconti-Sforza Tarot Cards*. New York: George Braziller, 1986.

Frye, Northrop. *Anatomy of Criticism*. Princeton: Princeton University Press, 1957.

Goethe, Johann Wolfgang von. *Faust*. An abridged version. Tr. By Louis MacNiece. London: 1951.

Harris, W. T., ed. *Webster's New International Dictionary of the English Language*. Springfield, MA: Merriam, 1934.

Luck, George. *Arcana Mundi; Magic and the Occult in the Greek and Roman Worlds*. Baltimore: John Hopkins University Press, 1985.

Scott, Walter, ed. *Hermetica*, 4 vols. Oxford, 1924-36.

Schwartz, Hillel. "On Reading the Tarot." *Journal of Unconventional History*, I, 2 (1990).

Wirth, Oswald. *Le Tarot des imagiers du moyen age*. Paris: Tchou, 1982.

Yates, Frances. "In the Cards." *The New York Review of Books*. CA. 1980.